Th

GW00993595

Best

In

Gozo

Guide

2014

Published by Palatino

P

66 Florence Road, Brighton BN1 6DJ UK
PO Box 2 Ghajnsielem, Gozo, Malta

The small print

Little moves faster these days than communication and information and nothing, good or bad, seems to stay the same for long.

It is probably inevitable that between the writing of this book and its publication, and between its publication and getting into the hands of the reader, some things will have changed.

If so it will obviously be beyond the control of its contributors. The information in it was, as far as it was possible to ascertain, correct at the time of going to press.

The editorial team cannot be held responsible if, for example, any of the restaurants considered by them to be among the island's 'best' at the time of writing suddenly deteriorates. Or increase its prices. Or changes ownership. Or gets a new telephone number. Or amends its menu. Or switches its hours or days of opening. Or even if it closes down completely.

The reader can and should always ring in advance and check, and book, of course.

Equally, we cannot vouch personally for the authenticity of the history or the legends herein.

For the most part, we weren't there when those things happened.

But the information was culled from extensive research and from conversations with experts (even, sometimes, from contemporary and eye-witness accounts).

If we have got anything wrong, please let us know. And we will do our level best to improve the next edition.

Our email address is: **bestingozo@gmail.com**

PO Box 2, Ghajnsielem, Gozo

Contents

₄Credits

*The paintings that illustrate this Guide are by local artist **David Carrington**, an expatriate Englishman, retired on Gozo.*

www.gozogallery.com showcases all his landscapes and portraiture, past and present. Work available for sale can be seen there. To commission a specific work of art, please get in touch with the artist directly.

The BIG (Best In Gozo) Guide

Visitors to this island may well find restaurants and places of interest that are not listed in this *Best In Gozo Guide*. In fact it is more than likely that they will do so. After all, Gozo prides itself on being one of the world's 'best-kept secrets'...

But what we have endeavoured to compile is a list of only what we consider to be the BEST – that we recommend to friends – and we will be delighted to hear of recommendations for inclusion in later editions. Our email is: **bestingozo@gmail.com**).

There are more than 200 'food outlets' on Gozo. We have listed only thirty-four, based on the experience of a team of people, native Gozitans and ex-pats who live here or who visit on a regular basis.

If the reviews appear largely uncritical, it is because they were chosen on the basis that they are very good, or the best, for one reason or another. Our reviewers do not announce their connections with this Guide when dining at restaurants, they do not accept free meals, and whether or not a venue opts to advertise is irrelevant. Inclusion in this Guide is by invitation. Opinion is of course subjective, which is why extra contributions will be welcomed.

And what is good one year may not be as good next year. Chefs and waiters move on; places deteriorate. They also improve. The list is intended to be a moveable feast, but it is hoped that inclusion in the Guide will encourage our nominated restaurateurs to maintain their already high standards.

If you, the reader, report a bad experience we will pass it on, and we will check later that any shortcomings have been amended (or we will consider whether the place still merits inclusion). And where appropriate we will report back to you.

Kul bl-aptit! – *The Editorial Team*

₆**Welcome to Gozo**

Gozo was always a destination for the traveller, rather than the tourist; people came to the island, basically, because nobody else came. In comparison with most Mediterranean islands – and especially with Malta – it had little traffic, was cleaner and greener, it was ideal for walking and its clean clear waters were excellent for diving; there were a few beautiful beaches plus a surprising amount of 'culture'.

It has changed a bit, over the years. Certainly there is much more traffic (more cars, it is said, than people) but some roads that were little more than farm tracks have improved beyond recognition.

The scenario started to alter when the Maltese woke up to the realisation of the little gem that they had on their doorstep, a 25-minute ferry ride away. It isn't the travellers who have changed, or who have changed Gozo – it's the Maltese who, in their thousands, have adopted the island as their weekend and holiday home.

This is beneficial to the economy in that it keeps businesses ticking over, out of season. Importantly, it means that some restaurants that used to close as soon as the foreigners left can now afford to keep running, and staff employed, all year round (although, fairly obviously, there are fewer places open in the winter months).

And tourism, local and foreign, is Gozo's biggest industry. The farmers and fishermen rely on the tourist market to sell their wares; the village shops and supermarkets sell both to tourists and to the people who earn their wages serving visitors. The schools educate the children of parents who work – directly or indirectly – in the tourism industry. There is no part of the island that isn't touched by this business.

The natives are friendly. You may find their driving a bit erratic but they are always happy to welcome visitors and make them feel at home: to share their island paradise.

Emergency number: Telephone **112** and immediately tell the operator that you are on Gozo – otherwise you will be connected to Malta's emergency services (and they cannot redirect your call).

Gozo General Hospital: 2156-1600. Look for the sign saying *Isptar Generali*. The name was recently changed from the original and actual name, presumably to accommodate all those visiting Maltese who for the last 40 years had experienced difficulty in understanding the word 'hospital' in the language of the people who paid for it and built it.

Taxis: Make sure that the meter is switched on *after* you have entered the cab, or agree on a price for the journey *before* getting in. Prices are displayed at the airport and at the ferry terminal.

Electricity is expensive and is 220-240 volts, similar to the UK, but less reliable. Three-pin UK plugs fit the system (visitors from elsewhere may need an adapter). Note that most electrical goods are still sold fitted with only two-pin plugs.

Directory enquiries: 1182 for local numbers; 1152 for overseas.

Disabled access: The footpaths of Gozo were not designed for wheelchairs, nor even for pushchairs and are virtually impossible. Most hotels and restaurants are becoming much more wheelchair-friendly.

Driving licence: A 'full' foreign driving licence is acceptable.

Sun lotion: The temperature is higher and the sunshine more fierce than anywhere in northern Europe. Wear sunscreen, and a hat.

Clothing: Women cover their shoulders before entering a church; brief shorts are not acceptable. Men should not be bare-chested in the streets. Nude and topless sunbathing is (officially) illegal, but unofficially accepted on some secluded beaches. (There used to be notices telling people to put on a raincoat before leaving the beach.)

8 Safety

Teenagers leave discos and hitch lifts home in the early hours, sometimes returning about the same time as their parents are leaving the house for Early Mass. That is one sign of how safe Gozo is perceived to be.

A highly visible police force (110 officers), especially in Victoria, and more discreet in the villages, ensures that the island is virtually free of street crime: no muggings, no pickpockets, no violence.

There has been only one car stolen in living memory. You might think it's because there is nowhere to go with it. But in this instance the miscreants were taking it to Malta. They were stopped by police and arrested before they reached the ferry.

Gozitans generally leave their keys in the front door of their homes, and their cars unlocked (although some say this changes at weekends and in August – 'when the Maltese come over').

But generally the island is considered to be crime free.

The older generations, at least, have not taken readily to the banking culture, preferring to keep their wealth hidden, especially from the tax collector. There are few ostentatious signs of wealth – a ring or two, a crucifix on a gold chain, is about as far as most of them go,

The dilapidated garden door in a wall, unpainted for centuries, may hide a sumptuous palazzo within.

It is a gentle, peaceful, contented way of life. It's the way Gozitans like it and are trying to keep it.

Travellers, often aged themselves, quickly notice the lifestyle and learn more about it and they appreciate it, too.

For many of them, it's one of the reasons for coming back.

Speaking the language[9]

Most Gozitans speak good English, some of them excellently. A large number of them have lived and worked in the UK, in Australia, America or Canada.

Nevertheless, many visitors like to know a few common words and the natives will be flattered (and possibly amused) if you make even a small effort.

The roots of the language are a result of the history: originally Arabic with contributions from Italian, French and English.

Hello *bongu* (bon-jew)
Good morning *bongornu* (bon-jornu)
Good evening *bonasira* (bona-seera)
How are you? *kif int?* (kiff int)
Thank you *grazzi* (grahtsy) ...**very much** *hafna* (haff-na)
How much? *kemm* (kemm)
I beg your pardon *skuzi* (skoosy)
Please *jekk joghgbox* (yekky-ojh-bock)
Yes *iva* (eeva/eewa)
No *le* (lay)
Now *issa* (iss-a)
Early *kmieni* (k'mainy)
Late *tard* (tard)
Where *fejn* (fain)
Inside *gewwa* (jo-wa)
Outside *barra* (barra)
Give me *tini* (teeny)
Tomorrow *ghada* (ahda)
Cheers *bis-sahha* (biss-sah-ha)
Lager (local) *Cisk* (chisk)
Worse for drink *fis-sakra* (fiss-sack-ra)
Goodbye *caw* (chow)

10**Food**

Gozitan food is a mixture of flavours and traditions inherited from and influenced by its many occupiers, from the Phoenicians to the British, by its geographical position (between Sicily and north Africa), and by the delicious and often abundant local produce.

Some restaurants serve a complimentary plate of *antipasti* which might include olives, *zalzett* (coriander-flavoured local sausage), *bigilla* (broad bean paste), sun-dried tomato and *galletti* (local crackers) with crusty local bread and olive oil. Gozo cheese (*gbejniet*) is small and round and can come fresh, soft, marinated or hard and peppered. It is also used as a filling for *ravioli* and *pastizzi* – the triangular flaky-pastry snack which sometimes contains peas as an alternative – or as a topping for *ftira* (flat sour-dough bread something similar to a pizza).

Local tomatoes are fantastic and exported by the ton. Italians, who know a thing or two about tomatoes, rate them highly for their flavour and prefer the Gozitan product for their salads and sauces. They appear as the major ingredient in the better British varieties of bottled tomato sauces and soups. Potatoes are also highly sought-after, easily rivalling those from Cyprus or Jersey. Gozo honey is greatly prized.

Local bread is simply unmatched, although it should ideally be eaten on the day of purchase (a Gozitan would not look at yesterday's bread).For meat, it is impossible to beat local pork. And fish – wild not farmed – obviously could not be better or fresher anywhere than it is on Gozo, where nowhere is more than ten minutes from the sea. Visitors should try *lampuki*, the favourite local fish, when in season (from mid-August).On a cool evening try a bowl of *minestra*, a thick vegetable soup. But no visitor should come to Gozo without also trying *aljotta* (al-yotta), the traditional spicy fish soup.

However for many visitors the most important ingredient on Gozo is the natives' natural hospitality.

Wine snobs used to sip Gozo wine carefully and describe it as 'an acquired taste', but in recent years the better labels have become a remarkably easy taste to acquire.

Vines were planted on Gozo's verdant valleys with wine presses built beside them more than 3,000 years ago. Across those three millennia it has progressed slowly from rough local 'farmers' wine' to a standard for the best quality varieties with its own legal and recognisable DOK – Denomination of Origin.

The most important vine-growing areas are the Ramla and Marsalforn valleys, cutting from south to north and creating a temperate micro-climate that, with loving care and attention, is producing high-quality wines.

Diners are recognising this and increasingly opting for wine that has been cultivated, harvested and pressed on the island.

The local soil and cool north-westerly or westerly winds produce a slight bitterness in the aftertaste which is unique and creates a character that is both robust and balanced. Some experts say they can taste very slight traces of salt – perhaps because the vineyards are so close to the sea – which is a bonus in enhancing the flavour.

'Maltese' wine relies to a large extent on grapes grown on Gozo, a fact acknowledged by the celebratory three-day **wine festival** in **Nadur** at the end of the harvest.

Nearly all the restaurants in Gozo show 'local' wines on their list, usually at the front, before the Italian, French and New World labels, and diners are experimenting – as of course they should – and discovering new and enjoyable tastes. And then they are taking bottles home as souvenirs of their holiday, because they are difficult to source back home.

12 Opera

It is a source of considerable pride to Gozitans that their island (population about 25,000) supports two opera houses while neighbouring Malta (about 420,000) has none. In fact the Royal Opera House in Malta was bombed by the Luftwaffe in 1942 and although Britain provided finance for its rebuilding, the money mysteriously disappeared. Seventy years later the debate continues about whether it will be rebuilt.

Gozo's two opera societies grew out of rival band clubs and now attract some of the world's best performers, usually from La Scala (Milan), Covent Garden (London) or the New York Metropolitan, backed by excellent local choirs and musicians.

The splendid opera houses are both on Republic Street in Victoria, a short walk apart.

The main annual operatic productions (there are other concerts during the year) are held in October and are usually quickly sold out, despite tickets costing up to €80.

This year's productions will be celebrating the work of Guiseppe Verdi, a great local favourite. The Aurora Theatre will be performing *Il Trovatore* on Saturday October 11. The Astra will present *Nabucco* on Thursday October 23 and Saturday October 25.

Being rivals they don't communicate or cooperate as much as opera lovers wish they would. Opera buffs would prefer the two events to be closer together, ideally no more than a week apart, with more than one or two performances by each society. This way, they point out, Gozo would effectively have a week or ten-day international opera festival that would attract audiences from all over Europe.

It would also offer frustrated music-loving visitors a greater opportunity to acquire tickets for the performances.

Thousands of people come to Gozo every year just to dive in the crystal clear waters around the island. Some come to learn, some to pursue their hobby, some to qualify for a PADI certificate; others come to teach. Some come for only a one-day dive as a new experience. Diving is available all year round in water that is warmer in winter than the air temperature in most of mainland Europe, and visibility can be 40m.

There is as much to see among the vibrant colours underwater as there is on land – dramatic reefs, tunnels, 'chimneys', arches and caves, amazing drops, fantastic rock formations, scuttled ships (one of them in fairly shallow water for inexperienced divers or even snorkelers) and wrecks... and fish: amberjack and barracuda, octopus, bass and bream, groupers and flying fish.

Courses are offered for all levels, from children trying out their first experience of scuba diving in less than six feet of water (with specially designed children's equipment to suit size and stature), via accompanied and 'autonomous' (solo) diving, to qualification as a Dive Master. All the equipment is available to hire, from fins and masks to underwater digital cameras. Everything is meticulously and hygienically cleaned after each use.

Specially built and equipped dive boats ensure that the entire island, plus the island of Comino and the north shore of Malta, can be readily accessed – usually within little more than fifteen minutes from your start point. But there are also opportunities for 'shore diving' – popular sites like the Blue Hole and Inland sea are accessible from land.

Some divers nowadays book ahead on email to guarantee that the equipment they'll need will be ready and waiting for them at the dive shop on their arrival and so that they won't waste valuable diving time.

St. Andrew's Divers Cove, situated in picturesque Xlendi Bay on the south-west coast of Gozo, offers a full range of diving and tourist services plus a fully-stocked dive shop with quality equipment at special value prices.

Divers, from beginners to professionals, can find the assistance they need, in a variety of languages, to fully appreciate diving around Gozo and Comino or to gain diving qualifications.

Services on land include airport transfers, accommodation and car hire

Contact Mark, Joe or Diana:

St. Andrew's Divers Cove
www.gozodive.com
St. Simon Street, Xlendi, Gozo, XLN1302 Malta
Tel: (+356) 2155-1301

standrew@gozodive.com

www.gozogallery.com

*Gozitans have been 'farming' salt around the coast for centuries –
certainly at least from the time of the Romans.*

*The sea spray is blown over the levelled out rocks and into shallow
trays, all carved out by hand. Then the water evaporates in the heat
of the sun to leave a covering of salt for the locals to collect.*

*Walkers encounter the 'salt pans' most frequently on the shores of
Marsalforn and Qala – but are asked to avoid stepping into them.*

*Once collected, the salt is cleaned and put in jars for storage or for
sale.*

*Tourists regularly buy Gozo's sea salt as gifts or as a souvenir of
their visit that can be put to practical use back home.*

It probably comes as something of a shock for people who have heard that Gozo is famous as a centre for walking to discover that there is not even a footpath from the ferry.

But then Gozitans do not walk on pavements; they can't because they are impossible and impassable and wave up and down like a roller-coaster, partly to accommodate domestic garages on a car-obsessed island, partly because houses build out onto them, and most likely because the planners are incapable of drawing a straight line. So they walk – when they walk at all – in the road.

In fact the locals don't go anywhere, as they quaintly put it, 'by walk': they go by car, and park as near to the door as possible. They used to do the *passagiata* – a stroll to the local belvedere or down to the harbour – in their best Sunday clothes; now they do it by car... sometimes three generations and a dog in one vehicle.

It's visitors who do the walking – off-road and usually between villages. There are plenty of country and coastal walks to choose from, and no shortage of books of maps and routes, most of them graded according to length, difficulty and theme.

The island's reputation as a walkers' destination is well deserved. There is so much to see: lush valleys and flat-topped hills, hidden bays and coves, oddly shaped rocks and caves, prehistoric temples, the watch-towers of the Knights, cathedral-sized village churches made of honey-coloured limestone, the sea, the salt-pans, the terraced vineyards and olive groves ... And along most routes there will be citrus and bamboo and the fragrant air of rosemary, thyme and fennel at your feet.

There is, at the time of writing, an excellent bus service that will get you back home. Nowhere on Gozo should involve a bus journey of more than about half an hour.

Giant Women

Ggantija *(Jee-gan-tee-ya)* is famously the oldest free-standing man-made structure in the world, predating the pyramids (2700-2100BC) and Stonehenge (3100BC); that is the important historical bit. The interesting element is that, according to legend, Ggantija (3600-3200BC) was not man-made at all, but woman-made.

The *Gganti*, so it is said, were a race of giant (ten to twelve feet tall – and skeletons have been found that prove it) women who would carry their children on their breasts and huge rocks on their backs and shoulders.

It was, so far as is known, built before the invention of the wheel, so how did they shift the megaliths – some of them five metres long and weighing more than 50 tons – that they couldn't possibly carry?

The answer may be that they invented the ball-bearing. Spherical stones were found near the site that would most likely have been used to help manoeuvre the massive rocks. Some say they originated in Sicily but that would involve a journey of more than 60 miles. There is no shortage of huge rocks on Gozo, as anybody who has seen the trucks hurtling through **Qala** and **Ghajnsielem** to the docks would readily confirm. But geologists say they are most likely from **Sannat**.

The buildings are believed to have been temples of a kind, and burnt animal bones excavated on the site may have been sacrifices but presumably might also have been burnt (or cooked) for food. It also provides evidence that they had discovered fire.

Whatever they are, they represent an extraordinary and unique cultural, artistic and technological development in an otherwise prehistoric period of human life.

Artefacts found at the site include two stone heads, a large stone block with a snake relief, and 'a phallic symbol'.

The Island Of Joy

Phoenicians thought the island of Gozo was pretty much circular and therefore resembled the shape of their round merchant ships, so they gave it the same name: *Gwl* (pronounced *Gol*).

The Greeks had a word for it: *Gaulos*; it was actually the Greek for Gwl and referred to the same type of ship. The Romans made only a minor change, to *Gaulus* (round vessel) and the Byzantines called it *Gaudes*, and sometimes *Gaudos*.

The Arabs phonetically transcribed it into their own language and into a word that, back-translated in a Roman alphabet, would be spelt *Ghawdex*.

The mediaeval Church latinised the name of the island as *Gaudisium* – which also happened to mean Joy.

When the Spanish took over they translated the Latin version into Castilian and decided that the word should be *Gozo*. It also meant joy, pleasure, delight, and also merriment and cheerfulness.

Many visitors would consider this to be hugely appropriate.

But by this time the natives had lost interest in what foreigners wanted to call their homeland. Ignoring everybody else they decided that *Ghawdex* (pronounced *Ow-desh*) worked for them. They reverted to it and have stuck with it ever since.

Similarly, when the capital city was renamed Victoria, in honour of the queen's jubilee in 1887, the Gozitans (they may call their island Ghawdex, but they call themselves Gozitans) stuck to *Rabat*, which in Arabic means suburb (of the walled Citadel).

And in 1964 when the Maltese renamed Gozo's main piazza as Independence Square, the locals decided that they preferred the old name of *It-Tokk*: the meeting place. And that is what they still call it.

Calypso's Island

It doesn't matter that Calypso was a mythological creature – a golden-haired nymph who lured the fabled Greek hero Odysseus (Ulysses) away from his wife Penelope and detained him on 'the island of Ogygia' for seven years. The story, in Homer's *Odyssey*, may (who knows?) be based on truth.

And, if it is true, then it is fairly obviously the case that 'Ogygia' was actually Gozo and the cave into which the nymph's enchanting singing lured the adventurer is just above the beautiful sandy bay called Ramla and is reached via the road through **Xaghra**. (The beach itself is most comfortably accessed via **Nadur**.)

With a modicum of imagination it is possible to make the facts fit the story.

The fable has a happy ending – at least for Odysseus. He appealed to his patron, the goddess Athena, who got in touch with Zeus, father of all gods, who sent his winged messenger Hermes to tell Calypso to set her hero free. And the nymph, who had promised the wanderer immortality if he would stay with her, relented and provided him with wine, bread and the wherewithal to build a small raft.

It is thought that the cave is the start of a labyrinth of tunnels leading down to the beach, but if so the route has been blocked by fallen boulders.

As caves go, it isn't particularly impressive, but the attraction is the magnificent view over the spectacular red sand beach of Ramla, and of course the feeling that one is communicating with Greek gods or at least with one famous goddess and one literary hero.

On the shore below the cave are the remains of **Marsalforn** Tower, built by the Knights in the early eighteenth century to protect against seaward invasion from the north of the island.

Why Gozo?

An interview on Maltese television with **Revel Barker** for the programme *Ghax Ghawdex?* – Why Gozo?

'I was born and started work in a big industrial city in the north of England and spent most of my holidays in cities. Then I visited Gozo on a job, stopped my hire car on the belvedere in **Ghajnsielem** and I think my life changed at that moment.

It was probably the first time I had looked at, and appreciated, scenery and 'a beautiful view' (that's what belvedere means). And I decided, there and then, that this was a place I'd like to retire to... even though I was only 29.

I came back frequently for holidays and in the meantime travelled widely – five times round the world – on business. But the island kept drawing me back. When I took early retirement I could have chosen almost anywhere to live, but I had never found anywhere to beat Gozo.

It wasn't only the natural beauty of the place, nor even the weather; the people were the deciding factor. So laid back as to be almost horizontal: happy, friendly and eager to be helpful. Tell them you have a problem and they will solve it for you – if they can't, they'll have a brother-in-law or a cousin who can.

Their driving is reckless; their understanding of parking and road signs is non-existent. Second-hand cars are sold with indicators 'as new'.

Their neighbours on 'mainland' Malta dismiss them as rural and uncultured – which as a criticism is both unfair and untrue, except that traditionally they rely to a large extent on the products of land and sea. But if you can translate uncultured as unpretentious, it's about right.

They are magic. I have lived in lots of places and I have never been happier, or felt more at home, than I do on Gozo.'

© Viewingmalta.com

Gozo is obviously busiest in summer – but at its most attractive (most people think) in what they call the 'shoulder months', at either end of the main tourist season. Usually light rain rapidly changes the colours from brown to green as it refreshes the fields. Occasional heavy downpours – and it seems an interesting and incredibly civilised fact that on Gozo it tends to rain most heavily only at night – refill the river courses that have been parched for several months.

The air is fresh and redolent with herbs, flowers spring forth, ramblers stroll about in comfort, farmers can till their fields which are no longer hard as concrete. It's the best time to visit: you can get a table in a restaurant... and there will be space to park your car.

'Independent' Gozo²³

The Romans arrived on *Gaulos* (Gozo) in 218BC and ran it as a *municipium* (free town) independent of Malta with its own government minting its own coins. The **Citadel** and its environs were known simply as *Gaulos Oppidum* (main settlement) – effectively the island city of Gozo.

The Knights (1530-1798), who had been given Gozo in a package that included Malta and the uncontrollable stretch of African Barbary coast known as Tripoli (Libya), ruled the two islands as one entity, albeit with one of their number as governor of Gozo, supported by a local council.

When they surrendered the islands Gozo had no official form of government, not even by the French, who didn't venture often outside of the Citadel and **Fort Chambray**, both of which they had occupied.

After only four months (on October 28, 1798) – discreetly assisted by Sir Alexander Ball, one of Nelson's commanders – the Gozitans' constant harassment of the occupying forces drove them out. More than 200 French soldiers agreed to surrender without a fight and handed the island, along with 24 cannon and ammunition, and 3,200 sacks of flour, back to its by then 16,000 inhabitants.

Malta was still occupied, and would remain so until the Royal Navy drove out the French in September 1800. Gozo was independent again. The island revolt had been orchestrated by a priest, Canon Francesco Saverio ('Saver') Cassar, from **Ghajnsielem** (in those days part of the parish of **Nadur**) and he became effective governor.

Invited by the Maltese to govern (and defend) the islands the British took the whole archipelago including Gozo under their control to form what was known as the Malta Protectorate. It became a crown colony in 1813 and achieved independence in 1964.

The Knights and Gozo

The track record of the Knights Hospitaller of St John is less impressive than their over-romanticised history might suggest.

They lost Jerusalem, and then the rest of the Holy Land to Saladin and his successors (1291); they were kicked out of Rhodes by Suleiman the Magnificent in 1522; they lost Gozo to the Turkish fleet in 1551 and Tripoli in north Africa the same year; and they surrendered Malta and Gozo to the Napoleonic French in 1798 without a shot being fired.

Their one notable success was the Siege of Malta (1565) which they nearly lost to Suleiman's forces because they had forgotten anything they had learnt during the crusades and occupied low-lying areas around Grand Harbour, leaving the high ground of Mount Sciberras (later Valletta) for the Turks to rain down shells. Only last-minute intervention by a Spanish-led relief force ended the siege after three months. It arrived at the time when the Grand Master had been forced to sit in an armchair, sword in hand, ready to face the final defeat.

Officially soldier-monks who took vows of poverty, obedience and celibacy (but not of chastity), when they were not controlling native slaves building grand palaces and watch-towers they led a mainly sybaritic life, eating off silver plate and generally carousing, posing in their fine clothes and gleaming armour, and taking local women (sometimes three generations of one family) as concubines.

As the historian Edward Gibbon put it: 'the Knights neglected to live, but were prepared to die, in the service of Christ.'

They sailed regularly across to Gozo for hunting with dogs and falcons. The **Barrakka** (where Gleneagles now stands) was the base at which they would await the ships for their return journey, in a hostel with stables and a store-room for wine (while they were waiting).

The Invasion: 1551

Among the titles held by Suleiman the Magnificent (1494-1566) were King of Kings, Emperor of the East and West, Majestic Caesar, Allah's Deputy on Earth... Possessor of Men's Necks...

He wanted to add Possessor of Malta to that string. In July 1551 he sent his formidable fleet and 10,000 men to attempt it but they failed. Rather than return empty handed they crossed to Gozo (population about 6,000) and besieged the **Citadel** which eventually capitulated.

Around 300 people escaped by climbing down the walls but were rounded up later in the fields. The rest, including the governor and a small band of Knights, were carried away to Tripoli and into slavery. The Turks flattened the church (St James) in what is now the main square and they spared only a priest and forty very elderly Gozitans.

Concerned that, uninhabited, the island might fall prey to Muslims, the Pope and the Knights invited Sicilians who wanted the chance to own land to move to Gozo and claim it. A few took the opportunity, bringing sheep, goats, cattle and wheat. It explains why there are today so many Sicilian surnames on the island; it also explains why Gozitans are still basically different from their neighbours on the south island.

The Sicilians also brought with them their love and loyalty for family, friends, village and island home (more or less in that order) that persist strongly to this day.

Nevertheless it was some 150 years before the island population reached the pre-1551 figure.

The Turks made later attacks on Gozo – in 1613 and 1709 – both of which were unsuccessful. In 1565 the Turks made their final attempt at attacking Malta, this time with 200 ships and 40,000 troops.

The Knights employed slaves to 'shave' the sides of Fungus Rock to make it impossible to climb, but the 'fungus' was so highly prized that people still tried to steal it, in spite of the penalty for even attempting to gather the plant being three years in the galleys.

The blood-red tuber continues to flourish there – in spring, having benefitted from winter rainfall – but unhindered by humans, on the tiny rock island that protects and shelters the deep-water Dwerja Bay, once believed to have been a massive cave, and at one time considered a safe haven for pirates scouring and plundering European merchant shipping on the main sea route from Europe to the African coast.

Fungus Fact and Fable

It's said that the Romans carried the blood-red tuber from Gozo into battle and used it as a styptic – it appeared to stop bleeding. The Knights also used it medicinally and valued the plant so highly that they made gifts of it to the supportive crowned heads of Europe every year on the feast of their patron, St John.

As far as it was then known the 'fungus' was unique to its home on the 180-ft high rock at the entrance to the deep lagoon known as **Dwerja** Bay and the Knights chipped away to smooth the sides and make climbing from sea-level impossible. Access was restricted to use of a wooden cart attached by cable from the mainland cliffs to the top of the rock and was under permanent guard by soldiers.

Because of its bulbous shape the Knights named it *Fungus Melitensis*, the Maltese Mushroom. Not surprisingly stories of its healing power – everything from amputations to erectile dysfunction – spread around the world.

Enter the scientists. First, they proclaimed, it wasn't a fungus at all but a parasitic tuber that siphoned nutrients from nearby plants. Second, it was not unique to Gozo, but grew all over the place, from Lanzarote to Afghanistan, Saudi Arabia and Iran. Third, it had no health-giving properties whatsoever.

But more recent research suggests that the foot-long tubers from 'Fungus Rock' may indeed have some medicinal benefit.

Current analysis appears to indicate that extracts of the herb may inhibit HIV, actually improve (not restrict) blood-flow and may lower blood pressure. There might even be a hormonal effect that would confirm its effectiveness in treating impotence.

So the Romans and the Knights got it mainly right – while being slightly wrong.

_{28}The Most Important Visitor

On June 22 1883, while tending her flock on the outskirts of **Gharb**, Karmela (Karmni) Grima, a shepherdess, heard a voice calling her from the fields into a tiny chapel that was dedicated to the Virgin Mary.

Terrified and trembling, she entered and was told to say three Hail Marys. The voice appeared to be coming to her from a painting of the Assumption of St Mary that hung inside the chapel. It then said: 'Remember me.'

Whether it was a question or an instruction is lost in time. And whether the testimony of this 45-year-old spinster was believed from the start when she first confided in her confessor is also unknown. But the Church eventually decided that the encounter represented a genuine visitation by the Blessed Virgin Mary.

The shrine quickly became a destination for thousands of pilgrims as a Marian memorial and in 1931 a new romanesque basilica was consecrated on the site of the chapel at Ta' Pinu, the area named after an early procurator of the original chapel, Filippino (Pinu) Gauci.

Aided by a €320,000 EU grant, Karmela's house, on the main road into Gharb, is now a museum with an audio-visual presentation (and two lifts). It also provides an insight into rural life in 19th century Gozo. Karmela died in 1922.

The shrine, later designated as a 'minor basilica', is decorated by mosaics with 76 coloured windows, and claims many miracles, as the stacks of votive walking-sticks and crutches seem to testify. On his visit to Gozo in May 1990, after praying privately in the chapel, Pope John Paul II celebrated mass on the parvis of 'The Shrine of Our Lady of Ta' Pinu' and decorated the statue of the Virgin with five golden stars.

St Mary's wish was granted: she has been remembered.

Falcon Facts

Most people know something about the 'Maltese Falcon', if only because of the (historically inaccurate) 1941 movie of that name, starring Humphrey Bogart and Peter Lorre.

The presentation of a falcon as tribute to King Charles V, the Holy Roman Emperor, every year on All Saints' Day, was the sole rent required for the Knights' perpetual lease of Malta, Gozo and Tripoli from 1530 to 1798. The islanders, who had organised a whip-round in order to buy their independence from the King, considered the deal, and the modest rent, to be both treacherous and insulting.

The birds – peregrine falcons – were actually bred not on Malta but on Gozo, mostly along the cliffs at **Ta' Cenc**. Reaching speeds of up to 200ph, they are thought to be the fastest in the world. The Knights used to cross to Gozo to engage in falconry, a favourite sport.

The falcons were housed in the village of **Xewkija** in a *barumbara* ('pigeon loft'), a former historic building that was 'accidentally' demolished and later used as a site for development.

The last falcon seen on Gozo was a male, illegally shot by Maltese hunters from a speedboat beneath the cliffs in 2012. The breeding female had been similarly shot and killed two months earlier.

Such, sadly, is the way the Maltese revere their islands' history, their heritage and their ecology.

Reports of the barbarism of renegade hunters have severely split the population of the islands into pro- and anti-hunting camps.

Efforts by a dedicated police unit to stamp out illegal shooting have been largely ineffective. But successive governments have been loath to act against the hunters because of the size and apparent voting power of the pro-hunting lobby.

30 The Luzzu

(Lut-soo, singular; *lutsy,* plural.*)* The gaily painted fishing boats in the harbour and often seen around the coast of Gozo will – if they are pointed at both ends with prominent bow and stern posts – be *luzzi.* If a boat is cut off squarely at the back it's called a *kajjik* (kayak). The *dghajsa*, a small open harbour boat originally propelled by a standing oarsman, like a Venetian gondola, but now more likely to be motorised, is less frequently seen in Gozo but enjoys a similar ancient history.

Most small fishing boats have a pair of eyes on the bow, said to be the eyes of Horus (an Egyptian goddess), or of Osirus (ancient Greek), and are believed to guide fishermen first to the best place for a catch, and then to see them safely back home.

The colours, traditionally stripes of yellow, red, green and blue used to denote the village where the owner lived. Now, although rarely changed, they are a matter of personal choice.

The luzzu design is thought to date back to the Phoenicians and has survived because of its sturdy reliability and fitness for even stormy local waters. Originally propelled by sail, they are now almost all diesel-powered, often with three drives.

Gozo-built boats are considered to be the most prized although these days they are also being crafted in moulded glass-reinforced plastic.

The luzzu is one of the emblems of island life and used to feature on the nation's coins.

Some have been converted for use as tourist boats, mainly for short sea trips because there are no facilities on board, but most are still in use for fishing.

Malta and Gozo have fourteen public or national holidays – more than any other country in the EU.

Nowadays not all the shops are shut – it is advisable to check locally – but banks and government offices and services will be closed.

When national holidays fall at weekends the holiday may sometimes be taken on the following Monday.

Wednesday January 1	New Year's Day
Monday February 10	Feast of St Paul's Shipwreck
Wednesday March 19	Feast of St Joseph
Monday March 31	Freedom Day
Friday April 18	Good Friday
Thursday May 1	Workers' Day
Saturday June 7	Sette Giugno
Sunday June 29	Feast of St Peter and St Paul
Friday August 15	Santa Marija
Monday September 8	Feast of Our Lady of Victories
Sunday September 21	Independence Day
Monday December 8	Feast of the Immaculate Conception
Saturday December 13	Republic Day
Thursday December 25	Christmas Day

32 Village Festas

Locals refer to the season of bells, yells and smells. Every village has a *Festa* during summer to commemorate its patron saint. The church bells chime almost constantly for at least three days and sometimes for a whole week. There will be fireworks (even during broad daylight when they can't be seen). The villagers go out to enjoy themselves and hawkers sell cooked food from trailers and stalls.

The parish church and the streets leading to it will be decorated with colourful lights and flags. A statue of the patron saint, and sometimes of other saints, is brought out of the church and carried through the streets, often accompanied by petards (loud explosions) and by the village band – most villages have their own band club.

There is a strong element of competition in that every village wants its festa to be better than that of the last village to celebrate. To the tourist the most apparent feature of festa life is likely to be the noise. In addition to the bells, the non-stop fireworks and the bands, there will almost certainly be dancing in the streets, until late at night.

Gozitans don't think they are enjoying themselves if they can hear each other speak.

Many village festas also include horse-racing in the streets, sometimes with jockeys saddled but more often in sulkies or racing rigs. The roads, obviously, will be closed to traffic while these events take place.

In theory it is the time for villagers to renew their religious vows, but it is more than that. It is a village and family get-together; an annual celebration. Many Gozitans who have emigrated – to England, the United States and even as far away as Australia – will often return in order to attend their own festa.

Visitors are always made welcome. The locals are eager to share their love for and loyalty to their village.

Festa Dates

Most festa days are fixed, but they may vary slightly according to the calendar. It is always advisable to check locally. Some village shops and restaurants may close during Festa Week. Some restaurants close early to allow staff to attend their festa.

May
Munxar – Feast of St Paul – last Sunday.

June
Għasri – Feast of Christ the Saviour – first Sunday.
Għajnsielem – Feast of St Anthony of Padua – second Sunday.
Fontana – Feast of the Sacred Heart – third Sunday.
Xewkija – Feast of St John the Baptist – on the Sunday nearest June 24.
Nadur – Feast of Saints Peter & Paul – on June 29.

July
Għarb – Feast of the Visit of Our Lady to St Elizabeth – first Sunday.
Kerċem – Feast of Our Lady of Perpetual Succour – second Sunday.
Rabat (Victoria) – Feast of St George – third Sunday.
Sannat – Feast of St Margaret the Martyr – fourth Sunday.

August
Qala – Feast of St Joseph – first Sunday.
San Lawrenz – Feast of St Laurence – second Sunday.
Rabat (Victoria) – Feast of Santa Marija (St Mary) – August 15.
Żebbuġ – Feast of St Marija – third Sunday.
Għajnsielem – Feast of Our Lady of Loreto –last Sunday of August.

September
Xlendi – Feast of Our Lady of Mt. Carmel – first Sunday.
Xagħra – Feast of the Nativity of Our Lady – September 8.
Rabat (Victoria) – Our Lady of Graces – second Sunday.

www.gozogallery.com

All Gozo life revolves around, or wends its way through, the capital (and only) city of Victoria with its beautifully prominent Citadel, Rabat (the suburb) and It-Tokk (the main square).

It is the cultural (two opera houses, a handful of museums), commercial, shopping and administrative centre of the island.

Go back far enough in history and it was also the seat of independent government for the island – on more than one occasion.

Carnival

Even the *Kunsill Lokali* of **Nadur**, which organises the main Gozo version of Mardi-Gras, readily admits that some people 'detest' its annual Carnival – 'when the silliness, the senseless and the idiotic takes over'... ('while others love it'). It is a long (ten-day) and noisy event involving often grotesque fancy dress costume, floats, street theatre, dancing and drinking going on late into the night. For some it marks the end of winter; officially it is the run-up to the start of Lent.

It comes in two parts: the first, on February 23 this year, is known as the 'organised' Carnival and starts around lunchtime in the main square of St Peter and St Paul. The second, called 'spontaneous' (or totally disorganised) section starts at sunset every night from February 28 to March 4. There is little let-up in between.

People flock to it from all parts of the island and from Malta and some even from abroad, giving cause for the claim that the Nadur Carnival is nowadays 'world famous'. Although allowing for the fact that most of the world hasn't even heard of Gozo, 'world famous in Gozo' might be a more accurate description.

Love it or hate it, the village will be chock-a-block with revellers intent on having a good time, most of them staggering about holding plastic drink containers (glasses are banned, for the duration). Streets will be closed; traffic wardens will be everywhere looking for an easy buck. There will be nowhere to park and not even much space to walk.

The Nadur Local Council while thanking all those involved in the organisation of the carnival [and] helping make this popular event such a success, asks... those attending to respect public order and decency and not offend public morality, to respect the laws of the country and take all precautions to avoid unnecessary accidents.

That says it all, really. Enjoy!

August 15 is the biggest day of the year on Gozo, by far outdoing even Christmas and Easter as joyous celebration with fireworks, bells, music, marches, dancing in the street, copious drinking... and more fireworks.

Santa Marija (the religious significance may be obscured by the partying, but officially it celebrates the Assumption to Heaven of the Virgin Mary) is the ultimate Gozitan **festa**.

The day is significant to Catholics all over the world, but people come to Gozo from all over the world to enjoy it here. It is a week-long holiday with offices and factories (but not food shops) shut for the duration.

The streets of **Victoria** will be thronged with people (and closed to traffic); the ferries will be packed with tourists (south-island Maltese and foreigners). There will be horse-racing on the main street during the day and religious processions at night.

Everywhere there will be fast-food and drink outlets and stalls selling (basically tatty) children's toys.

The day-time temperature in August can be 32-38C (at night averaging 24C) and the sea temperature probably 26C. The heat-absorbing limestone buildings will have been gaining baking heat for a couple of months.

In other words, it will be hot.This is vital to remember if you are planning to arrive on Gozo during that week. The ferries may run a shuttle service if they think the queues for the regular time-table are getting out of hand. But it would be wise to prepare for a long wait.

It is advisable to take a bottle of water and sunscreen to preserve your sanity while waiting at Cirkewwa... before losing it at the festa.

Wine festival

The grape harvest ends in August-September and is celebrated on Gozo with a massive and jolly three-day party in **Nadur**.

It is organised by a fourth-generation Maltese winemaker possibly unique in that it is a winemaker without vineyards: its grapes are grown on Gozo and pressed in Malta. So the event provides an opportunity for their contracted growers to get together when their annual toil is over.

There are nearly 400 of them, most with little more than a handkerchief-sized vineyard chosen on the basis of soil matched with grape variety, the slope of the land and the grower's trellising, planting and pruning techniques. The vines are meticulously monitored during the growing season by experts from the winery in order to ensure the best flavour, consistency and quality. It works: the wines have won more than 80 international awards.

The public are of course welcome to join in the party and experience different local grape varietals.

Visitors simply purchase a souvenir glass and then move around the festival asking for it to be refilled as often as they wish, and with as many different wines as they find that they want to sample. (The following evening, they are welcome to buy another souvenir glass and start all over again.)

There is live entertainment and food – typically roast suckling pig, oriental dishes, pasta and of course the 'national' dish: rabbit – available from a number of stalls or in a seated dining area with a view across the Gozo Channel (the festival takes place on the village's belvedere which commands one of the best views on the islands).

This year's party will be on August 29-31, from 7pm to 11.30 (with the intention of closing around midnight).

Room At The Inn

For the past five years the village of **Ghajnsielem** has produced the biggest and best 'Nativity Play' in the Mediterranean, in Europe, and possibly in the world.

One hundred and fifty actors, performing on a five-acre site, recreate the town of Bethlehem as a living crib – complete with 'Baby Jesus' – for four weeks every Christmas.

Local volunteers have constructed a working village, with a stream and a water wheel providing power for threshing, a field of crops, a duck pond and a farmer's tool shed.

There are village and shepherds' houses, a working farm, a baker producing fresh bread, blacksmith, market-place, carpenter, crafts shop and a tavern that serves beer and its own-label wine.

There is even an inn, appropriately called The Star. And in the past it has been possible stay in it. It is worth enquiring; then, with a bit of planning, you could spend Christmas in Bethlehem, while on Gozo.

More than 75,000 people visited the site last year (2013-4), making Bethlehem-in-Ghajnsielem the most popular tourist attraction on the Maltese islands. Official visitors from the other Bethlehem (in Palestine) have also visited, and approved.

The spectacle closes in January with Epiphany and the arrival of the Three Wise Men on horseback from the East.

They used to start their journey in Malta, in order to arrive from 'overseas'. This year they started in Rome, in St Peter's Square, taking in a visit to Tolfa, Ghajnsielem's twin town a few miles outside the Holy City and coming 'from the east'.

Next year... who knows?

The Heart Of Gozo

The newest addition to the cultural story of the island is a bright clean white-walled museum dedicated to the fascinating (mainly religious) history of Gozo. Its alternative name is il-Hagar (*eel-hajar*) which basically means hewn stone, but used to describe a settlement with a boundary wall of stone: a community.

Converted from three town houses in Charity Street, on the left of St George's basilica in **Victoria**, it has an unevenly stacked 'spine' of local indigenous stone running through four floors as a timeline for the cultures and civilisations of the island and their different forms of art, materials, languages and attitudes, from the pre-historic **Ggantija** through Punic, Roman, Byzantine, Islam and European – the **Knights**, the French and the British – to the modern day.

Indeed, the latest 'artefacts' include the mitre and skull-cap of the last Pope (Benedict) and the cassock that was being worn by the present incumbent (Francis) at the moment of his election to the Papacy. (It may be no small coincidence that Monsignor Alfred Xuereb, the private secretary to both Popes and now the Vatican's economics minister, was a Gozitan – from *San Gorg tal-Hagar*, in Victoria.)

There are some other fairly modern as well as ancient examples of local religious art, but the bulk of the exhibition is comprised of church treasures (including gold altar fronts and silver chandeliers) and a great number of donations from private collections – and therefore which have never previously been seen. The entire building, glass floored and glass-staircased, is wheel-chair friendly (there's a lift) and the tour takes about forty minutes, including audio, audiovisual and interactive exhibits.

There is also an open roof with spectacular views of the dome of the basilica, the citadel, most of the town of Victoria and the south eastern part of the island.

This (*the meeting place*) is a market place, a centre for *festi*, and sometimes a concert-square, where you'll be ambushed on arrival by hawkers desperate to sell straw hats or sunglasses, flick knives or towels, shorts or skirts, fresh vegetables and fish... and coffee.

When Independence Square (its official name, never used, is *Pjazza Independenza*) is not in use for a set-piece celebration it is the place for coffee and often remarkably wholesome and tasty snacks at tables set out within a barricade of merchants' stalls. And, as its unofficial name implies, for meeting friends.

It is edged by tall clipped ficus trees in which birds known locally as 'Spanish sparrows' sit all day and drop messages onto the cars parked beneath. Taxi drivers awaiting fares on a small rank in the corner usually drape sheets over their vehicles, more as a defence against the birds than against the mid-day heat.

It's a great place for people-watching – long files of day-tripping tourists in new straw hats trailing behind a guide holding a parasol aloft – and waiters dodging skilfully through the constant stream of traffic on the island's main road to serve your food and drink. Or for leaving your chair for a couple of minutes to make purchases from the fishmonger, chemist, greengrocer, souvenir shop, dressmaker or from the shop selling traditional Gozo food.

The history is there, too. The island's War Memorial in the centre; to the right the semi-circular *Banca Giuratale* which once housed the *Universitas* – the largely self-governing council of the island led by a *hakem* (ruler); on the left a bust of Saver Cassar, hero of the revolution against the French, and the church of St James the Apostle, where the bells used to be rung so violently to drown out political (Labour Party) speeches in the square that the structure of it started to collapse. The original building had been flattened by Turks in the raid of 1551.

42 Gozo: The Movie

Victoria's Citadella Cinema, at the bottom of Castle Hill which leads up to the Citadel itself, is currently undergoing a modernisation programme for big feature movie screenings.

But meanwhile there is a splendid must-see attraction on show... a spectacular sound-and-vision experience of the history, culture and beauty of the island in *Gozo 360°*.

In about half an hour it displays more than a thousand pictures of 'Calypso's Island', its past as well as its present-day life.

It will prompt visitors to add places to their proposed itinerary as well as probably suggesting the perfect camera angles for the souvenir photographs of their holiday in Gozo.

If you didn't know and love the island before you entered the cinema to watch this entrancing screening, you will do both when you leave it.

The cinema is air-conditioned and comfortable and commentaries are available on headsets in Italian, Danish Dutch, English, Finnish, French, German, Greek, Hebrew, Hungarian, Japanese, Maltese, Polish, Russian, Spanish, and Swedish.

It is open daily (except Sundays when it opens only for pre-booked group audiences) from 10am-3pm with screenings every half hour.

The cinema can also be accessed via its bar on the main street. There is disabled access and a lift.

GOZO 360°

Island of Joy

"A spectacular show!"

Opening Hours
Monday - Saturday - 10.00hrs - 15.00hrs
Public Holidays - 10.00hrs - 13.00hrs
Sundays open on request for groups

 CITADEL CINEMA

Tel no.: 21559955
www.gozo360.com.mt

Sight-Seeing

The new (to Gozo) method of exploring the island is on double-deck open-top busses with hop-on hop-off tickets so that when passengers spot a location of special interest they can leave the bus, have a look round and catch the next one to continue their journey. There are two different routes, departing daily every 45 minutes from Mġarr Harbour; they last about two hours and a one-day ticket is valid for both routes. (Make a note of the time of the last daily circuit.)

The tours take in such tourist attractions as Ramla Bay, the Ġgantija Temples and Xagħra Windmill, Calypso's Cave, Marsalforn Bay, Ta' Pinu Basilica, the Crafts Village, Azure Window (Dwejra), Fontana, Xlendi Bay and Xewkija. So they provide the perfect opportunity for sight-seeing, shopping and even for swimming.

Tours end back at Mgarr Harbour and pass by the Victoria Bus Station a number of times.

But the other way to see Gozo (and Comino) is by sea. A sea trip offers an entirely different aspect to the island.

Charter a yacht (or share the price) or take a motor cruise from Mgarr.

Depending on the wind strength and direction it is possible to circumnavigate both islands in a day's sailing on a skippered 47-foot yacht with a glass of wine in your hand and anchoring in sheltered bays for snorkelling and swimming in the clean clear water that surrounds the islands. Or book to cruise romantically at sunset.

Or take a cruise to the historic Grand Harbour in Valletta on a three-engined locally built 52-ft wooden motor cruiser... or cross to Comino for an evening barbecue in Blue Lagoon.

It's the crews' ambition to make your sea trip the most memorable day of your holiday.

SAIL GOZO
Sailing Adventures

Private Sailing Charters
Sunset Sailing Tours
Gozo, Comino, Malta

Sailing in Gozo and Comino

Setting off from Mgarr Marina in Gozo we take a gentle sail along the stunning coastline to call in at one of the bays of Comino and the Blue Lagoon for a swim and relax, followed by a freshly prepared meal with a glass or two of wine. Beautiful secluded bays, great scenery, warm tranquil cyan waters, all make for that perfect relaxed day. .

SAILGOZO.COM   00356 7956 1526

The Citadelx

On a clear day from the top of the bastions, as is also possible from the heights of **Nadur** and of **Xaghra**, you can see Sicily, 60 miles away and, when it erupts, the flames of Mount Etna which is still active.

A Punic (Carthaginian) inscription found on the site indicates that the Phoenicians and Carthaginians who had colonised Gozo around 550BC built temples, partly fortified, on the summit of the Citadel hill.

The Romans (218BC) had created their acropolis there, with a township beneath its walls. Under the Knights, who arrived in 1530, development of the fortress continued following the disastrous siege of 1551 through to the 1690s and although buildings have naturally deteriorated (and are being slowly restored) little has changed since that time.

The modern defences were happily never tested although they appear impregnable, with a natural bluff on the north topped by a circular medieval wall, a bare slope and ditch that would deny cover to any invading army, and a 270-degree gun battery. The present covered entrance was formerly a drawbridge that was raised every night.

What visitors often fail to notice are the entrances to two 'sally-ports' – tunnels built for the movement of troops out of the fortress, complete with tracks for the carriage of ammunition boxes.

The Citadel houses the Cathedral, law courts, and museums devoted to local archaeology, folklore, natural history, armoury and the church. There is also the small prison where Jean Parisot de Valette, later Grand Master and saviour of Malta in 1565, was imprisoned for a time for duelling with a fellow knight.

The view from the ramparts is stunning, across rolling valleys and flat-topped hills with Malta to the south and – on a clear day – Sicily to the north.

_{48}Rabat (Victoria)

The island's capital (and only) city – all the other communities are villages or parishes; there are no towns – Rabat (meaning *suburb*) is a centre of mainly small shops and balconied houses based around the slightly off-centre square called *It-Tokk*.

Its maze of narrow streets and alleys in the old part of town (*il-Borgo*) twist and turn deliberately, to baffle invaders and deflect the flight of arrows and gunshot.

One third of all the churches on Gozo are within these city limits.

Behind It-Tokk is another square, *Pjazza San Gorg*, graced by St George's basilica. For Rabat has at least two of everything. It even has two opera houses (Malta, they will tell you, while trying to hide their pride, has none – the Royal Opera House in Valletta was bombed during the war and nobody can remember where the money went that was donated by overseas governments for its rebuilding.)

Rabat is very much an administrative, cultural and commercial hub. The Ministry (of Gozo) is a few hundred yards away, as is the general hospital (*Isptar Generali*). The police headquarters, main post office, the banks, the Bishop's palace, two large supermarkets, the semi-circular *Banca Giuritale* (from where the island used to be governed) and the opera houses are all on the main road (Republic Street).

Car parking, frustratingly for Gozitans who don't care much for walking, is a couple of hundred yards away from just about everything.

The two main churches (Santa Marija in the Citadel and St George in the 'suburb') nowadays make a truce at Easter, holding their massive Good Friday celebrations on alternate years. Otherwise St George celebrates its own festa on the third weekend in July and St Mary celebrates on August 15. In both cases it's a riot of dancing, drinking, eating and firework displays. This is, after all, the Island of Joy.

Fort Chambray⁴⁹

Picture the scene: the Grand Master summons the Admiral of the Fleet into his impressive palace in Valletta and orders him to stop attacking and plundering Turkish ships. The Knights have effectively been at peace with the Turks for some time, he explains.

No, replies the Admiral (Frenchman Jacques Francois Chambray, or de Chambrai). Attacking Turks is what the Knights do, and have always done. And while he is in charge it is what the fleet will continue to do.

All right, Jacques, says the Grand Master (Portuguese Antonio Manuel de Vilhena). When you came into this room you were Lieutenant-General of Ships; when you go out of the door you will be governor of Gozo. Or so the story goes.

Jacques doesn't appear to have been made governor, but in 1722 he embarked on an ambitious building project to create a fortified and impregnable city, along the lines of Valletta, at the entrance to Gozo.

The new city-fort at **Mgarr** was effectively the first speculative building on the island. The law (not taken too seriously by the locals) required all Gozitans to return to the Citadel every night for safety. Chambray's intention was that his development would be bigger, better and safer than the Citadel, and that families would buy homes within it.

He invested the fruits of his plunder and left money in his will but the scheme failed – mainly because since his fleet had stopped attacking Turkish shipping there was little or no risk of invasion.

Completed in 1760 the fort's importance soon diminished and it was abandoned for many years. Under British rule it was used variously as a hospital, a barracks, a mental institution and a leper colony. But following independence it was sold, for more spec building, and most of its historic architecture allowed to be demolished.

Gozo has forty shades of blue: more than even the most skilled water-colourist or the most modern camera could capture. You see them best from the balcony of Gleneagles, the (predominantly) fishermen's bar on the harbour. The blue hulls of the **luzzi** reflect in the blue waters of the shallow port; the sea mirrors the bright blue sky; different depths have different tones; whenever a boat moves, the shades change. Across the channel and its swirling currents the **Blue Lagoon** on **Comino**, with a seabed of golden sand, has its unique hue.

You note Gleneagles when coming in to port on the ferry; the building is *il-barrakka*, the waiting-room. It is described by most people as the best pub on the island and by some as the only proper pub.

The first recorded Gozo-Malta ferry was in 1241: the jetty is still there, beneath the pub's balcony. There was already an *osteria* (tavern) on the site in 1732 when it was rebuilt for the Knights. The bar is named after the first (1885) powered ship employed as a ferry. *Gleneagles* operated a twice-daily passenger and mail service to Malta, and (from 1892) a weekly run to Siracusa, Sicily, until 1914.

Bombed by the *Luftwaffe* during the last war and rebuilt in 1942, the bar's double-height ceiling, strewn with fishing nets and bamboo fish-traps, makes the place cool in summer and freezing in winter. Its walls are decorated by stuffed fish, luzzu propellers, and photos of old Mgarr. Owners Tony and Sammy serve draught beer, lager, Stella, Guinness and Gozo Brewery Ale. They will even make a Pimms in summer. There is a coffee machine, but no food.

But the balcony is the place to be – either for the joy of a sundowner while watching the constant movement of boats, for waiting for the ferry (you see it come in and prepare for its outward voyage, then walk the few yards to buy a ticket and board it). Or just for trying to count the different shades of cyan.

Comino

What happened to Gozo – independent 'travellers' being replaced by package tourists – has happened even more dramatically to Comino, the beautiful, barren and virtually uninhabited island sitting (once) peacefully in the channel between Gozo and Malta.

In the 13th century its population was a single Spanish hermit, a philosopher called Abraham Ben Samuel Abulafia, who wanted to unify Jews with Christians and then both with Muslims. When he tried to convert the Pope, Nicholas III, to Judaism he was condemned to be burnt at the stake but the Pope died and the sentence was repealed.

In the 15th century the sheltered bays of Comino and its broken-away rock of Cominotto (little Comino) were a haven for pirates who found easy prey in the vital maritime communication between Malta and Gozo, and also among merchant ships crossing the Mediterranean. In 1416 the local people petitioned the Viceroy of Sicily to provide some form of defence for the tiny island and taxes were raised to pay for a fort but the money was spent elsewhere...Ninety years after their arrival the Knights eventually built St Mary's Tower – chiefly for their own protection against pirates and the Turkish fleet – and stationed a detachment of 30 soldiers there. Such safety led to the establishment of an agricultural community of around 200 farmers, trying to eke out an existence from fishing, growing cumin (from which the island got its name) and cotton, and producing honey. It is said that the Knights used the island for hunting hare and wild boar. But agricultural life on the island was unsustainable and, long after the Knights had left, the British occupiers used the now-deserted island as an isolation hospital during the First World War. A set of buildings became 'Liberty Square', complete with a grocer's shop and a bar. When the British left a Swiss entrepreneur built a hotel there, and the island was introduced to tourism.

Although inland the island of **Comino** has altered little through the centuries, within much less than a generation the beautiful bays around its coast have undergone what can only be described as a sea-change.

A sudden bout of conspicuous wealth – possibly brought about by the need to dispose of hidden Maltese liri with the advent of the euro – produced a fleet of yachts, luxury cruisers and speedboats, all looking for somewhere to go... and finding Comino's bays close at hand.

In Blue Lagoon in August, where fifteen years ago you might have found a couple of **luzzu** fishermen and maybe a lone French adventurer on a salt-crusted yacht, you could almost walk across the lagoon from Comino to Cominotto on the decks of white plastic boats anchored gunwale to gunwale.

Around the shore will be those ubiquitous trucks selling ice cream and fast food to tourists and hikers, and people renting out umbrellas and sun-loungers. Unless they are doing business there, Gozitans don't go near Comino in the height of summer. Tourists, of course, do.

It is still a great place to walk, along a few remaining farm tracks amid the cumin – which still grows wild in little clumps between the rocks – and the pink and mauve flowering thyme. It is only one square mile in area, so the rocky wilderness, the jagged cliffs, the small sandy beaches, the coves and creeks and rock tunnels can easily be explored within a single day.

The former Swiss hotel runs its own ferry service to Mgarr and there are water taxis that ply regularly from the harbour and can be booked individually for the short journey across the Channel. If you're not in a hurry the skipper may well take you around some of the intriguing caves on your journey home.

Astonishing
GOZO
accommodation

Villaġġ Ta' Sbejħa

GOZO
Village
HOLIDAYS

Villaġġ Tal-Fanc

(*Ein*, as in Einstein; *see*; *lem*.) The *Ghajn* (spring or fountain) now embellished by a statue of a goat-herd in Apparition Square, near the children's playing field, was near enough to the harbour to be used by ships to replenish their water supply. It may have been named after Selim, a Turkish naval commander, or alternatively could be from *Sliem* – peace – and thence the village would be the 'fountain of peace'.

The largest village in area – it encompasses the island of **Comino** – it is the gateway to Gozo and includes the harbour, **Mgarr**, and the fortress of **Chambray** from where visiting British troops introduced the game of soccer to the islanders.

There are four significant places of worship. The old church (Our Lady of Loreto, 1820) was constructed after the goat-herd, Anglu Grech, was instructed by a vision of the Virgin Mary to build a church close to the spring. The stunning gothic edifice dominating the harbour (Our Lady of Lourdes, 1888) was erected after a visitor pointed out the striking resemblance of the rocks on the hillside to the grotto of St Bernadette in Lourdes. The Franciscan Order built its own church (St Anthony, 1906). And a big new church was started in 1922 to meet the demands of an expanding parish.

There is also a small church (St Mary) on Comino that dates back to the 13th century (rebuilt in 1667 and again in 1716) and a disused chapel (St Cecilia) next to the tower of that name on the main road to **Victoria**, close to what used to be the heliport. As a consequence Ghajnsielem probably has more religious processions than any other parish: *Kwaranturi* (40 hours of prayer) on January 1; Our Lady of Sorrows (week before Easter); St Joseph the Worker (May 1); St Anthony's (July); Our Lady of Loreto (August); Our Lady of Rosary (October); St Julian (November); and St Andrew (December).

'Fountain of Peace' may therefore be something of a misnomer.

56Qala

(Arla.) A great place for walking – in fact the roads from any direction are so bad they are probably more comfortable for walking than for driving. One great walk is from the harbour at Mgarr, all the way along the south coast, with fields on one side, attractive rock formations and caves and hand-hewn salt pans on the other.

The main church for the whole south-east corner of the island used to be sited here, taking in **Nadur**, **Ghajnsielem**, **Mgarr** and **Comino** as well as Qala. Then a bigger church was built in Nadur and that became the parish 'seat' until the late 19th century when Qala and Ghajnsielem became parishes in their own right.

Qala means bay or harbour and the inclusion of Mgarr within its ecclesiastical limits may explain that. Otherwise it would most certainly refer to the much smaller bay at Hondoq ir-Rummein (Valley of Pomegranates – although there are not many to be found these days).

Hondoq is a small and pebbly cove favoured by locals. It looks directly at Comino and is a popular spot for swimming, diving and boat trips.

Admiral Nelson spent some time at the recently (part-) renovated St Anthony's Battery, further along the coast – at least long enough to write a letter from it to Lady Hamilton.

Even further along – possibly about as far as one might want to walk – is a big quarry producing high quality limestone which was used to build Gozo's war memorial, the Grand Harbour breakwater in Malta and later the Metropolitan Cathedral of Christ the King in Liverpool – the biggest Catholic cathedral in England. Several times a day heavy lorries rattle and roar through the otherwise peaceful village square of St Joseph ('The Worker') carrying huge rocks towards the port. But, lorries apart, Qala is a very friendly, busy, lively village with signs of activity and restaurants open all year round.

(Shah-ra.) A busy, bustling, friendly wide-open square with roads running off in all directions and locals parking apparently at random. It is dominated by a grand and imposing basilica with 20 stained glass windows and an awesome collection of paintings, silver ware, sculptures and marble work inside. The name means plateau and was formerly known as *il-Qacca* (highest place).

As a settlement it is ancient – no doubt about that, for it includes **Ggantija** (3600BC, the oldest free-standing structure in the world).But even older, though no longer 'standing' are the remains of the Neolithic Santa Verna temple. There are also bronze age relics in the village, others from the Temple period, and a huge monolith known as *Ta' Sansuna* (the feminine equivalent of Samson).

Xaghra is also – as if we were likely to forget – the one-time home of **Calypso** and Odysseus. But there are other caverns: Xerri's Grotto and Ninu's Cave are fascinating and intricate underground mazes of stalactites and stalagmites, both discovered by workmen digging out cellars for water collection and storage.

Good Friday has been celebrated for the past hundred years by a street pageant in which costumed villagers act out the Passion of Christ, from his prayers at Gethsemane and his betrayal by Judas to his burial and the tears of the Virgin. The performance continues through the weekend to the Resurrection and is regarded as the best enactment on the island.

Before the start of the narrow twisty road down the high cliffs to **Ramla** beach is the sweet little Church of the Nazarene, and opposite it one of the best village stores (a mini supermarket). The houses atop the cliffs tend to have large terraces and command views of the Ramla valley and beach, and north to Sicily. It is more or less the view that had attracted the nymph Calypso to the village all those years ago.

The view on a misty morning across the valley from Sannat church to the rotunda dedicated to St John the Baptist at Xewkija.

Completed in 1981 and paid for by the villagers, it boasts the third largest supported dome in the world. St Peter's in Rome remains the biggest; a church in Africa was forbidden to build a bigger one so created a dome only slightly smaller than St Peter's.

The Xewkija dome is 74 metres high, with a diameter of 27 metres and a circumference of 85 metres. Its total weight is calculated to be around 45,000 tonnes.

(*Show-kee-a.*) Its inhabitants will tell you that they are the longest-serving Christians and have the oldest Christian church in the world. And they believe that. Apparently they went down to the water's edge at Mgarr ix-Xini and could hear St Paul preaching, in Naxxar in Malta, some twelve miles away. So they trekked back up the hill to Xewkija, demolished a former Phoenician temple known as The Sheik's Chair (where the Romans venerated their gods Venus, Diana, Apollo and Juno), and used the stone to build a Christian church.

That would have been in 60AD. Since that time the site hasn't changed but the structure has been rebuilt several times. The current church, boasting the third biggest dome in the world, was built over and around the previous version before it was dismantled. It could accommodate a congregation of 3,000 – or virtually everybody in the village if they all turned up at the same time.

The Knights used Xewkija as their main base for hunting, which they mainly enjoyed along the neighbouring cliffs of Ta'Cenc. They built three towers there. One, the Gourgion Tower, was demolished in 1942 by American Cee-Bees (construction battalions) to make way for a runway preparatory to the airborne invasion of Sicily. It took less than a fortnight to build, a fact that has probably gone unnoticed by the modern roadbuilders of Gozo.

The occupation of the village is both industrial and agricultural. The island's industrial estate (still not fully occupied) is there, near the main road. So, further away, are the small farms and terraces of vines, olives, tomatoes and citrus fruit established by the Romans, or possibly even by earlier occupiers.

It is also, on its border with **Ghajnsielem**, the site of the former heliport which, some people believe, will be extended one day to become a runway for small to medium-sized commercial aircraft.

Marsalforn

Marsalforn is not a parish, nor even officially a village (it is part of the parish of **Zebbug**) but it is Gozo's biggest and busiest resort. *Marsa* means port; *lifurna* was an Arabic word for ship. But *forn* also means oven or bakery and there is a legend that invading pirates were once defeated and sent scurrying back to their ship after being pelted with loaves and bags of flour by girls employed by the harbour's baker.

Frantic in summer, almost deserted in winter, there are plans to build a breakwater to protect the bay from fierce north winds and tides and create a secondary main harbour; *il-Menqa* (minor port) has room for only a small number of fishing boats. The dried-up (except following heavy rain) river course was once an extension of the harbour.

Its church has some claim to being the oldest on the island. The date of an original building is unknown but it was built on the site where St Paul, it is said, stopped to preach before sailing from the harbour to face trial in Rome following his shipwreck on Malta in 60AD.

The coastline extends north to include Qbajjar (*By-ar*) and the salt pans carved into rocks along the shore, some of them Roman but most dating from the 18th century and still in use providing tons of coarse sea-salt that is highly prized by cooks.

Dominating the area is a hill and popular vantage-point originally called *il-Merzuq* (meaning ray or sunbeam) where a huge wooden cross was erected in 1901. It was replaced by a 12-metre-tall concrete statue of Christ and renamed *Tas-Salvatur* (the Saviour's Hill).

Marsalforn is about ten minutes drive from Victoria, yet a notable number of city dwellers keep a summer home there – as do several hundred people normally resident on Malta. The popularity of the bay among both locals and tourists justifies the number of good restaurants along the sea front, from *il-Menqa* to Qbajjar.

www.gozogallery.com

At the end of a long day spent fishing a luzzu returns to the safe harbour of the Menqa (Menn-ah), the tiny sheltered port on the island's northern coast at Marsalforn.

The fishermen's haven is on the right-hand side as you approach the bay and there is a police station, a hotel and a string of small restaurants right beside it.

There is a limited amount of car parking available there (sometimes closed to visitors in the high season) but you need to get there before the fishermen to find a space. Otherwise, there is an official car park.

Sannat

As a village it doesn't have much going for it unless you know that it is the location of Ta'Cenc (*ta-chench*), the dramatic 400-feet high cliffs from which the island's most famous hotel also takes its name.

Here you will find gouges in the rock that are widely believed to have been cart (or, more likely, sled) tracks. Mysteriously, there are similar and equally-spaced tracks on Sicily and Malta and even in Libya, which is cited by some as proof that there was an overland route from Italy to Africa before the great flood. The only problem is that the theory would rely on centuries of travellers, with no known navigational skills or equipment, taking exactly the same route for centuries, and not wavering from the track by as much as an inch, in order to score the rock so distinctly. However nobody has yet come up with any more plausible explanation for them.

The cliffs were the home of the Maltese **falcon** and have become popular for walkers who can spot different varieties of wild orchid in tiny patches of soil among the rock. Geologists have established that the rocks from which **Ggantija** was built were gathered from this location by the giant women who carried them on their shoulders (or, more likely, painstakingly rolled them).

Between Ta'Cenc and Xewkija is the deep valley opening on to Mgarr ix-Xini (*im-jar-ish-sheeny*), where the Turks anchored and loaded their captive Gozitans in order to take them into slavery during the invasion of 1551.

Local men farm the valley terraces and their wives still make fine and highly rated Gozo lace, vying with Xlendi as the home of the most intricate designs. The Queen, before the coronation and while she was a Navy wife and living on Malta, went to watch the lacemakers at a house in Sannat called tax-Xelina, and since renamed Lace House. The motto of the village is *Labor ante omnia* – work before everything else.

Some bright spark decided recently that Xlendi should become a port for use by cruise liners calling in at Gozo but the project was abandoned when it was pointed out that, first, the sea outside the limits of the harbour was too deep to anchor, second that the bay was a swimmers-only area in summer, so cruise passengers could not be ferried in, and finally that the narrow bay could not possibly cope with any more traffic than it has already during the tourist season.

So the normal approach to this pretty and popular resort with its imposing cliffs and parade of busy seafront restaurants is by land, through the bottleneck of Fontana with its historic wash-house and via a recently resurfaced road alongside the deep Xlendi valley to the bustling waterfront.

(*Shlendy*.) Near-impossible to find a parking space in summer, delightfully and beautifully peaceful in winter (except at weekends when people come down to the bay to eat) it is officially part of the parish of Munxar, a community that otherwise has nothing remarkable apart from its unusual peace and quietness all year round.

The ladies of Xlendi have for generations been at the forefront of the manufacture of Gozo lace and filigree work which has become famous around the world and you'll still see them sitting in their doorways practising their art.

Xlendi is a usually safe fishermen's harbour, protected by a statue of St Andrew, their patron saint, and sheltered by high white cliffs. It faces due west – producing the most gorgeous sunsets, right down the middle of the fjord-like bay.

Nevertheless it has had its moments. There was the time when an earthquake caused the sea to withdraw for more than a mile, then rush back violently, flooding the valley. But that was in 1693. More recently the valley flash-flooded and sent waves in the other direction, washing most of the cars in the carpark around the seafront buildings and into the bay. There was a 'high-water mark' in the old St Patrick's hotel, about four feet above ground level.

The Romans used the bay as a shallow harbour and the Byzantines named it, from a word meaning 'ship'. The Knights built a tower (1650) on the headland to protect Gozo from attack from the west.

In the Christian era the locals worshipped in a cave church dedicated to St Dominica and it was from there that a Gozitan nun, Karolina Cauchi, founded the now worldwide order of Dominican Sisters in 1889. The cave became known as *l-Ghar* (cave) *ta'Karolina*. She also raised funds to pay for steps to be cut into the rock to enable visitors to reach the top of the cliffs.

(Na-doer.) The name of this village is from an Arabic word meaning lookout and it is easy to understand why – it commands views to both north and south. And the tower on top of its hill was built not by the Knights but by the British, for semaphore, and later telegraphic, communication with Malta.

Its selection by the EU as a 'European Destination of Excellence' in tourism may surprise people at first glance. The roads to the village and inside it are among the worst-kept and worst lighted on the island (which is saying a lot). The centre is wide and spacious but generally unremarkable; there are excellent village shops and two cash machines but no hotels and only one notable restaurant, on the outskirts.

With 5,000 inhabitant the second largest community (after Victoria) on the island, it celebrates Carnival in great style and its wine festival with great noise but that, surely, can't be sufficient to merit such an accolade from Brussels, can it?

No: it is the beaches that are outstanding. San Blas and Ramla are by far the best on the archipelago. Maltese Tourist Authority's advertising may not mention Gozo at all, but the photographs it uses will be of the beaches for which Nadur is the gateway.

San Blas is a pretty sandy beach, sufficiently isolated to have become popular in parts for (theoretically illegal) nude bathing for those who want it. It involves a giddy walk down a steep rough path between tamarisks and citrus trees and bamboo plants, and an exhausting walk back. It is actually far more easily accessible from the sea.

Ramla, the red sandy beach on which Odysseus was washed ashore on his epic return from Troy is far bigger and is accessed by a new road which in summer will be lined with cars. There are two cafes on the beach, and hawkers providing sun-beds, umbrellas and windbreaks. Nadur is, then, an 'excellent' destination...

The road from Victoria was announced as being the first road ever to be built in the Maltese islands that would be completed on time and in budget. That was six years ago; the 3km road was still being worked on this year and the cost (85% funded by the EU) has gone up from nearly five million euros to just short of nine million.

The part that has been finished is good. But the importance of the road is that it leads to some of the most interesting tourist places on the island. It also leads to a five-star hotel, but was like a cart track for the last few hundred yards.

San Lawrenz itself is tiny – a village square with a few short streets. Literary buffs may know that it was the last place Nicholas Monsarrat (*The Cruel Sea, The Tribe That Lost Its Head*) lived and where he wrote *The Kappillan of Malta;* one of the streets is named in his honour.

Dwerja Bay is believed to have been a deepwater cave before its roof caved in. Its entrance is guarded by **Fungus Rock**, home of the 'Maltese mushroom'. Dwerja Tower was built in 1651 to defend both the plant and the bay from pirates. There is also a smallish body-length cave that, on a summer night, would have accommodated one guard.

The rocky coastline features hundreds of visible fossils of creatures ranging from tiny lizards to enormous sharks.

At the other end is the Inland Sea, a pebble-beach crater surrounded by cliffs and boat houses connected to the Mediterranean by a 60-metre long multi-coloured tunnel through which local fishermen will ferry tourists to see the other spectacles.

These include the Azure Window, a rock structure that has become a favourite subject for photographers. Situated as it is at the extreme of the archipelago it is considered by many to be nature's 'gateway' to the islands. All it needed was a decent road.

(*Asry.*) In terms of population the smallest village on the island, it is dominated by the Gordan lighthouse, 180metres above sea level and visible for 50km. It is the last navigational point for long-distance sailors before Gibraltar.

The name of the village probably means olive-press (Zebbug, next door, is from an Arabic word for olives).

It is in a gorgeous valley between impressively high cliffs, popular for walkers and cyclists, especially in winter and spring when the paths lead between typical Gozitan farmhouses (several of them available for holiday lets) and lush green countryside dotted by fragrant and colourful flowers and herbs. The valley opens into the sea at a beautiful calm and secluded pebbly little inlet about 300metres long and greatly favoured for swimming, snorkelling and diving. It is teeming with marine life.

There are a number of underwater caves, perhaps the most impressive being a vertical shaft from the top of the cliffs to the sea, where residents used to lower buckets to fill with seawater to replenish their cliff-top saltpans.

Following the coast brings explorers via Zebbug to the busy coastal resort of **Marsalforn**.

The lighthouse, which commands a 360° view of the island, was built by the occupying British for the Royal Navy in the 1850s on a site that had been used as a lookout for northern invasion since Roman times. Originally oil-fuelled, and later illuminated by 23 gas-burning lamps, it was converted to electricity in the 1960s.

Archaeologists have found evidence of human life in the valley dating back to 4500BC. More recently, onyx has been discovered on the slopes facing the lighthouse.

(Arb.) The name means West, and is about as far as you can drive from the ferry without falling off the edge. The parish includes the basilica of **Ta' Pinu** and the house of Karmela Grima.

Although it has become a popular residence for ex-pats who are prepared to face the obstacle of **Victoria** every time they want to go anywhere, you rarely see people on the streets. This may be because it is so difficult to get in and out of.

It is at the (completed) end of the Victoria to **San Lawrenz** road, and so far so good, but becomes a bottle-neck at the start of the village. At the far end, centre of the village in the main square, there is an eccentric 'roundabout', difficult for long vehicles to manoeuvre.

The square is dominated by a flamboyant late 17th-century baroque church in the style of Francesco Borromini – who gave the style its name (the original is in the Piazza Navona, in Rome). Dedicated to The Visitation of Our Lady, symbols of faith, hope and charity are carved around the main door in a striking concave facade.

A great place for religious legends, the best in Gharb is undoubtedly the story of St Demetrius (a patron of the Crusades who had a small church built in his name) and a woman called Zgugina. Her only son Mattew was snatched from the shore by pirates. She saw it happen, rushed into church and appealed to the portrait of the mounted saint for help. He leapt out of his painting, galloped across the water in pursuit of the departing galley, slew the pirates and carried the boy safely back to his mother's arms.

Typically, Zgugina pledged to keep an oil lamp burning for ever in front of the saint's portrait. But in time the church crumbled and fell into the sea. And – here is the bit that gives confidence to the deeply religious – scuba divers and fishermen who have explored the site report that the lamp is still burning...

Village shopping

Some villages (but by no means all of them) have a village store or 'mini supermarket', a greengrocer, butcher, baker, a post office and a chemist. A few will have a stationer's, probably doubling as a souvenir shop. One or two even have a video rental shop. A couple of villages have hardware stores, some have yacht chandlers.

There are no standard opening times although they tend to open early and close around 7pm. But most village shops will be closed between noon (or 1pm) and 4pm. Others may stay open all day, in theory, but if it's a nice day your friendly local shopkeeper might decide to spend the afternoon at the beach. Some shops open on Sundays and public holidays, at least in the morning; others take every available opportunity for a day off work.

Village stores do not take credit cards. There are cash machines at the ferry terminal, two in the excellent main square at Nadur, in the car park at Xlendi, on the seafront at Marsalforn, and at the main banks in Victoria.

Most village food stores sell a small range of beer, wine and spirits. Most will have at least a small selection of fresh fruit and vegetables

Among the best are: Abraham's Wine Cellar, opposite the Church of the Nazarene in **Xaghra**, with ready-to-cook food, cooked meat and a good range of wine; Cini, beside the main **Xewkija** cemetery, a butcher and general food store; the Lighthouse supermarkets at **Ghasri** and **Gharb**; Azzopardi in Said Street, **Nadur**, selling food, drink and household goods.

Fresh fruit and vegetables are sold at the farm estate shop on the road to **Marsalforn**.

There are greengrocers' trucks in the main car park in **Victoria**.

Shopping – general⁷¹

The big news for local shoppers on Gozo this year has been the opening of a 1,000-square-metre **Lidl** superstore on the outskirts of Victoria. Lidl fans will be familiar with its range, from lobsters to angle -grinders, from ankle socks to loaves of bread (although some travellers report that local prices are considerably higher than in the UK). It opens from 7am to 8pm and has parking for 100 cars.

There are two shopping malls, **Arkadia** and **The Duke**, both with food supermarkets, also in Victoria; both have limited parking and are open all day, most days. The non-food sections of these shopping centres will operate different hours. **Miracle** has a large choice of frozen food including imported joints of meat and poultry. **Ta'Dirjanu** and **Ta'Mema** are food and general supermarkets. All of them are on the main road between Victoria and the harbour.

The **Jubilee** shop in It-Tokk has a range of local produce ready to eat or ready to cook. **Vini e Capricci** (see over) specialises in gourmet and delicatessen foods.

The main outlet for fresh fish is **Bugeja** in Ghajnsielem, also on the main road to the ferry. But another shop (same name) recently opened round the corner off what used to be known as the 'heliport roundabout'.

Nearly all the chemists close in the afternoon. Although two, **Ghajnsielem Pharmacy** in Independence Square and **Gozo Chemists** on the main road past Xewkija open all day, except Sunday. *The Sunday Times of Malta* (if you can find somewhere to buy one) will list those pharmacies that are open on Sunday mornings, on a rota system.

There is a shop at Savina Square and another close to the main police station, both in **Victoria**, that sell local and some overseas newspapers daily and on Sundays, but parking is not usually easy at either of them.

Gourmet food

The aroma of fresh coffee and chocolate tempts you inside the newest and biggest speciality food and drink outlet on the island.

Vino e Capricci (it means wines and whims) raised the standard of Gozo supermarket and delicatessen shopping when it opened last year at the Agricultural Village just off the main Xewkija roundabout.

It is a state-of-the-art concept in more ways than one for it is a genuine work of art in itself, from its entrance with coffees, teas and chocolate, through cheese, cured meats, pasta and antipasti... the Gozitan selection of local products including oils, conserves, wines and liqueurs, where you can have your own bottle filled with local olive oil from a stainless steel vat...

Then on to its stone-clad temperature-controlled wine, sprit and beer cellar... There are twelve brands of quality Belgian beer and more than 1,000 different wines ranging from the local and European to the new world.

The section extends to an extensive range of dessert wines, fine brandies, grappa, calvados, rums, single malt whiskies, sparking wines and champagne.

Among the 'whims' are hand-blown glass napkin rings and ornaments, vases made from local glass and stone, paintings by Gozitan artists, wine holders and wine racks.

Essentially it is a gourmet paradise where, in many cases, you are invited to taste – and sometimes even to sample drink – before you buy the products.

Vini e Capricci is open for trade and personal shoppers from Monday to Saturday, from 9 am to 6 pm.

Getting Around

Quad Bikes and Jeeps: Hire a quad bike or jeep for a guided tour or to go it alone. Full instruction will be provided for beginners but a full (car) driving licence is required and you must be over 25. www.gozopridetours.com
2156-4776

Cycles: Rent a bicycle, mountain bike, moped, a scooter or a motorbike. from www.on2wheelsgozo.com
2156-1503

Horses: To explore the hills and valleys on horseback, or to learn how to look after horses and ponies, or even how to drive a horse-drawn carriage, contact Victor Muscat at www.vmcarriages.com
2155-9229

Self-drive motorboats: Can be hired at Xlendi for swimming, fishing, sunbathing, a picnic or a trip to a secluded beach. Bear in mind that local drivers are no better in boats than they are in cars, so stay well clear of other mariners. www.xlendicruises.com
9942-7917

Taxis: Fares are listed on boards at the ferry terminal and at the taxi rank on the corner of It-Tokk. Mini-cab fares are invariably cheaper.

Airport taxis: Book to be collected from your apartment or hotel direct to the airport with a local taxi and save the hassle of the ferry terminal(s) and tickets, and keep your luggage with you.

Depending on your start point it costs about €60.00 for up to three passengers – a good deal.

Otherwise, it's one taxi to the ferry at Mgarr, where you buy your ticket, then the hope of finding another one – or a bus – at Cirkewwa.

Door to Door
Direct Airport Transfers

Malta/Gozo Personal Tours

Cab & Minibus Service

Tel No: 00356 2156 4461

Joseph 00356 **9986 6698**

Carmen 00356 **9987 7668**

Buskett Str, Nadur,
Gozo - Malta
NDR 2241

Email: info@gozoway.com
website: **www.gozoway.com**

Best Way To Discover Gozo

Gozo Pride Tours offers you the opportunity to discover the hidden charms of Gozo.

A journey through the mysterious island of Gozo. Country Roads, Stunning Cliffs Breathtaking Views and all the highlights of Gozo are part of our Tours.

For more details contact us on :
Tel: 0035621564776
Mob: 0035699440845
URL: www.gozopridetours.com
Email: info@gozopridetours.com

Tours Available in Gozo
Full Day Jeep Tou
Full Day Quad Tou
Half Day Quad Tou

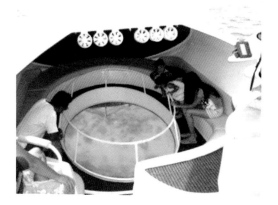

APOLLO UNDERWATER SAFARI
& BLUE LAGOON TRANSFERS.
Departure; Mgarr harbour Gozo from the main jetty.
For more information please contact, Angelo;
00356 99478119 or visit www.apollogozo.com

Hire Cars

Parking: Hire cars are identifiable by the number plate and are easy prey for traffic wardens who are paid commission and have a daily quota to fulfil. They know that they can expect no argument from tourists. Even a visitor who is on Gozo for an extended stay will find it unlikely that an appeal against the issuing of a ticket can be heard in time. Cases that come to court will be adjourned, often indefinitely, if the warden doesn't turn up. And the penalty (increased if not paid immediately) will automatically appear on the hirer's credit card bill.

There are no meters on Gozo and parking is generally free. Some parking areas require drivers to display a 'clock' in the windscreen, showing the arrival time. Even then it is not unheard of for a ticket to be issued by a warden who will say he didn't see it. So park with care. Park on the left, or bonnet-to-kerb, so that the warden doesn't need to step off the pavement. It is illegal to make them walk.

Accidents: If another driver is in the wrong, the chances are that he will suddenly lose the ability to speak any recognisable language. Do not move your vehicle until the police arrive (they are usually fairly quick on the scene) unless it is 'in a dangerous position'. You and the other driver will need to agree on the definition of 'dangerous'. The possible effects on other traffic are completely irrelevant. Take photographs of the scene – and the position of the vehicles in relation to the central white line (if any is visible). Carry your passport, hire agreement including insurance, and your driving licence.

Alcohol: the drink-driving limit is the same as the UK. Police can suspend your licence on the spot.

Speed limit: 50kph (30 mph) in built-up areas; 64kph (40mph) on 'open' roads, and 80kph (50mph) on 'unrestricted' roads.

Seat belts: Mandatory for all passengers

Driving, Gozo-fashion, should not be in any book about the best – except that in the list of really bad drivers of the world Gozo would come fairly near the top: the best of the worst. And it would be remiss of any guide book not to warn visitors about it.

One problem is the horse-and-cart mentality which still persists. Horses do not usually run into each other head-on, so steering was never much of a bother. They don't have mirrors or indicators. Also, you could dismount from a cart anywhere and the horse would normally pull it into the side of the road – so parking four feet away from the kerb was not a consideration.

The bigger problem, since cars started to replace horses on Gozo, has been the driving test.

Until recently the test involved passing between two oil drums, in forward and reverse gears, in a car park; but if this proved difficult the examiner would widen the gap. The test did not include any reference to parking, to the use of mirrors, indicators or lights, to hill-starts, emerging from side-roads, overtaking, or emergency stops, traffic lights, pedestrian crossings or roundabouts, to turning right or even on which side of the road motorists were legally supposed to drive.

(The Tourist Authority, asked on which side of the road locals drove, used to say 'the shady side'. They presumably thought that was funny.)

For the motor-cycle test you were sent out of the car park and round a roundabout and if you returned without having fallen off or hit anything you got your licence. When several examiners were found guilty of giving licences to people who had paid them, but not even turned up for a test, they were all given presidential pardons. There was a 98 per cent pass rate. It made experienced drivers wonder about the two per cent who failed.

Souvenirs – What To Take Home

From the farm shop:
Sun-dried tomato paste, sun-dried tomatoes, cold-pressed extra virgin olive oil, olives in brine, Gozo peppered cheeselets, pickled onions, Gozo honey, carob syrup, fruit jams (pomegranate, prickly pear, fig, orange, melon, apple, strawberry, plum), Seville orange marmalade, candied peel, prickly pear and pomegranate liqueurs and dessert wines, chutneys, wild capers in vinegar, Gozitan sweets and biscuits

From the Crafts Village:
A former British army camp, Gozo's Crafts Village is between Gharb and San Lawrenz and a great place to find genuine local souvenirs – many of which you can watch being made.

These include mouth-blown glass, hand-made lace, woollens, rugs, silver and gold filigree, limestone sculptures, marble, onyz and alabaster, pottery, paintings, rugs and leatherwork, sheet-metal art, costume jewellery and wood carvings.

'Duty free':
There is no longer any actual 'duty free' allowance within the EU, but the traditional items like wine, tobacco, cigars and cigarettes are still far cheaper on Gozo than in mainland Europe.

The wine limit for bringing bottles back to the UK was obviously designed for people taking vans to Calais and is hardly likely to affect the modern air traveller (10 litres of spirits, 90 litres of wine).

For smokers the limits are 800 cigarettes, 200 cigars, or 1 kg of smoking tobacco. The only requirement is that local tax was paid at the point of purchase (and that the goods are not intended for resale).

In St George's Square, Victoria, it is possible to find prices that are lower than those at the airport.

Ferry Times (Summer)

Sailing times may vary slightly, especially in the early hours, so it is advisable to collect a current timetable from the terminal at Mgarr.

From Gozo	From Malta
00.45 (Daily)	01.15 (Daily)
02.00 (Daily)	02.35 (Daily)
03.30 (Daily)	04.00 (daily)
05.00 (Daily)	05.45 (Daily)
06.00 (Daily)	06.30 (Mon-Fri, Exc. PH)
06.30 (Mon-Fri, Exc PH)	06.45 (Sat, Sun & PH)
06.45 (Sat, Sun & PH)	07.00 (Mon-Fri, Exc. PH)
07.00 (Mon-Fri Exc PH)	07.30 (Daily)
07.30 (Daily)	08.15 (Daily)
08.15 (Daily)	09.00 (Daily)
09.00 (Daily)	09.45 (Daily)
09.45 (Daily)	10.30 (Daily)
10.30 (Daily)	11.15 (Daily)
11.15 (Daily)	12.00 (Daily)
12.00 (Daily)	12.45 (Daily)
12.45 (Daily)	13.30 (Daily)
13.30 (Daily)	14.15 (Daily)
14.15 (Daily)	15.00 (Daily)
15.00 (Daily)	15.45 (Daily)
15.45 (Daily)	16.30 (Daily)
16.30 (Daily)	17.15 (Daily)
17.15 (Daily)	18.00 (Daily)
18.00 (Daily)	18.45 (Daily)
18.45 (Daily)	19.30 (Daily)
19.30 (Daily)	20.15 (Daily)
20.15 (Daily)	21.00 (Daily)
21.00 (Daily)	21.45 (Daily)
21.45 (Daily)	22.15 (Daily)
23.00 (Daily)	23.45 (Daily)

Dining Out On Gozo

Gozitan, Maltese (there's a subtle difference), Italian, French, Mediterranean, Chinese, Indian, Thai...Steakhouses, grills, barbecues, pizza ovens, flambés... Indoors, outdoors, beaches, gardens, rooftops, or take-aways... City, seaside, sea view, country view or no view...noisy, quiet, elegant or basic... intimate or vast.

Whatever you are looking for, whatever your preferred culinary taste at any particular time, you can find it on Gozo. There is even a McDonalds – which to some people is seen as a sign that 'civilisation' has reached the island.

The restaurants in this book were nominated by frequent diners as being 'the best' – for one reason or another. There are more than 200 'eating outlets' on Gozo (180 are listed in Trip Advisor). But these are the places the regulars recommend to visiting friends.

Whichever is your preference you are strongly advised to book to avoid disappointment. Mention (if you feel so inclined) that you found them through this Guide. They will be pleased to know that.

The price guide is based quite simply on the lowest price you are likely to pay for a simple three-course meal, and the most expensive dishes on the menu at the time the restaurants were checked. Opting for lobster (when available) is likely to hike the higher price up a bit. The price range does not include wine, water or coffee.

If you are concerned about food allergies, vegetarian or lactose- or gluten-free meals, please mention the fact when booking. If you ask a waiter and he appears unsure, ask to speak to the manager or the chef.

Smoking is forbidden by law in enclosed restaurants but usually allowed in the open air. As a general guide, if there is an ashtray on the table, smoking is permitted there.

Where to eat

Take-Away

Cafe Jubilee
D-Bar
Fliegu
It-Tokk
Oleander
Pings
Sapana
Seaview

84 **I-Ankra**
2155-5656
Local and international
11 Shore Street, **Mgarr**
Website:
Open: Daily 6pm-10.30. Sundays noon-10.30pm.
Vegetarian, Gluten-free meals available

Local favourite
Price range: €23-41
major credit cards

One of those restaurants that can be walked to from the ferry, a few yards up the hill, opposite the Gleneagles bar. It offers a full menu of the usual standard and Gozitan dishes, with the emphasis on different varieties of meat, especially tender quality steaks. But regulars are equally likely to opt for the specials, starters and main courses, which vary according to the best and freshest food on the market. They may also go for the specials in wine – the featured 'wine of the week' – which tend to favour good local Gozo-grown wines.

The restaurant occasionally organises theme nights, about once a month, including Spanish, Sicilian, French and Hungarian evenings. With a bit of notice they can come up with a theme meal of your choice. Ask about what is coming up. More than that: tell them what you like and they'll do their best to provide it for you.

The new owners, John-Paul in the kitchen, Gino front of house, are two young guys who are eager to ensure that their customers are satisfied by their provision of good quality fresh food, attentive service and comfortable surroundings. Nothing, it seems, is too much trouble for them.

Air-conditioned
Seats 50
Parking on street
Dress: Casual.
High chairs: well-behaved children welcome.

where passion meets expectation

where passion meets expectation

Ankra Restaurant
11, shore street
Mgarr Gozo
Bookings tel:
21555656
99869404

facebook / pages / Ankra Imgarr Gozo

86 Beppe's

2750-0567

Stylish dining

Price range: €23-48

All major credit cards

Italian, Mediterranean
Il-Menqa, **Marsalforn**
Website: www.beppesrestaurant.com
Open: 10.30-2.30; 6.30-10.30. **Closed Monday**
Vegetarian, Gluten-free meals available

Chef-patron Joseph Spiteri acquired his skills in some of the best restaurants on Gozo, with a couple of years in London, before opening his own venue beside the slipway of the tiny harbour in Marsalforn. He put a lot of effort into discovering what people really want to eat when dining out and then his aim has been to 'conquer the taste buds' with his cooking of it.

From baked brie wrapped n parma ham or pepper-crusted beef fillet carpaccio, his fresh mouth-watering antipasto misto, or pan-seared rabbit liver to grilled calamari, boneless quail stuffed with chicken mousse, prawn and scallop squid-ink ravioli, or sea bass with a prawn mousse roulade, there is likely to be a pleasant and welcome surprise in the taste of Joseph's food.

His brother Franklin, front of house, ensures that the quality of the food from the kitchen is complemented by friendly and attentive service.

Air-conditioned
Seats 65 inside, 50 outside (sheltered in winter)
Parking in area
Dress code: casual.

High chairs and baby-changing facilities.

Wheelchair access and WC.

AVAILABLE
NOW
REAL ALE
FROM
GOZO
LIGHT AND HOPPY
BREWED IN
GOZO
3.8% ABV
GOZBREWERY.COM

88 Boat House
2156 9153
Maltese and Mediterranean
Xlendi Bay, **Xlendi**
Website: theboathousegozo.com
Open: Daily, 12.30-1.00am
Vegetarian, Gluten-free meals available

Water's edge
Price range: €18-40
All major credit cards

Right at the water's edge at the very end of the road into the bay and next to the fishermen's statue of St Andrew, this well-located restaurant has great views straight out between the cliffs and enjoys the most wonderful sunsets.

Restaurateurs Joseph and Rose Attard run a well-organised team of efficient and attentive waiting staff and have created a thoughtful menu with an appealing range of dishes – more than a dozen different starters and antipasti, main courses enhanced by daily specials such as crispy suckling pig or lobster or creamy salmon and shrimp pancakes, in addition to the usual fare of pasta, a dozen salads, pizza, fresh fish and shellfish (the local *luzzi* are tied up immediately beside the restaurant wall), Argentinean or Irish steaks, chicken, and thin and crispy pizzas.

The restaurant has its own-label local olive oil and a wine list of more than 200 local, classic and new world wines.

It is likely to be busy all through summer and at most weekends even in low season, so book.

Seats 80
Parking nearby
Dress: Any
Children and babies welcome: high chairs available
Wheelchair access and WC facilities.

THE BOAT HOUSE

restaurant | mediterranean cuisine

XLENDI BAY - GOZO

reservations:
27567207,
21569153,
21557661

With "excellent quality and quantity always guaranteed" diners rate this as "one of the best in Gozo" to enjoy "great dining by the sea". "The cherry on the cake" for a weekend getaway.

90Café Jubilee

City bistro

2155-8921

Mediterranean and Local; café, bar, bistro

All major credit cards

Independence Square, **Victoria**
Website: www.cafejubilee.com.mt
Open: Mon-Fri: 8am-1am; Sat 8am-2am; **Closed Sunday**

A landmark eatery for Gozo, Café Jubilee has spread it wings from here, first to Malta and then as far afield as Budapest and Shanghai – proof of the brilliance of its concept.

Completely renovated this year, it remains styled after a Parisian bistro, perhaps lifted straight out of Montparnasse: the wood-panelled walls are covered with collectible bric-a-brac and prints of pictures and posters recalling the 1920s and 30s. It is narrow inside, so a bit like eating in a railway buffet car, but there are plenty of seats outside across the main road in the square known as *It-Tokk* and a couple of tables on the pavement.

Much more than a mere 'café', the accent here is on variety, taste and value for money with highly efficient and friendly service.

The pad-style menu features the regular favourites: soups, sandwiches, salads and pasta, the English breakfast... main dishes of salmon, chicken, tuna... home-made beef and ale pie and the delicious apple and sultana pie.

But the blackboard is the place to look because the fresh food available changes daily and sometimes several times during the day.

The bar has draught lager and Guinness and a range of local and imported beers. Next door is their shop, offering a splendid array of Gozitan produce including food that can be taken home for cooking.

Seats 35 inside; 32 outside
Air-conditioned
Parking: Main car park
Dress code: Any
Children and babies welcome

Il Carrubo
2219-1000
Italian
Ta' Cenc Hotel, **Sannat**
Website: www.tacenc.com
Open: Daily, 7-10 am; 1pm-2.30; 7.30pm-9.30.
Vegetarian, Gluten-free, meals available

Fine dining: Country
Price range: €30-48
All major credit cards

A table under the carob tree... for decades now the al fresco dining area at this five-star hotel has been regarded as the most romantic spot on the island. The 400-year-old tree is the place to be, if you can book it.

The hotel was closed for a month for restoration at the beginning of this year and reopened under the charge of the legendary Dr Rota who has returned (for a second time) as general manager inspired to recapture much of the hotel's heritage – it was created as a 'private' hotel to accommodate an Italian family's wealthy and elegant friends and the buildings and furnishings reflected and complemented their lifestyle: fitted carpets, chandeliers, marble floors...

The menu isn't merely à la carte, but *à la grande carte*. Simply reading it gets the taste buds going. Antipasto such as prawns wrapped in smoked salmon with a fresh mint mousse; mains including black angus steer fillet with a foie gras sauce or slices of veal flavoured with truffle; and flambéed custard crêpes for dessert...

But there is also a daily-changing menu at €30 with slightly more modest but equally tasty dishes that might vary from pasta to lamb cutlets, chicken breast and fresh tuna. Either way it's a dining experience.

Air-conditioned inside
Seats 200 inside, 200 outside
Car park
Dress code: Smart-casual.
Children welcome; high chairs available

Chez Amand
2156-1188

Seafront
Price range: €20-50
All major credit cards

Mediterranean, Local, French, Belgian
Qbajjar Bay, **Marsalforn**
Website
Open: lunch daily; dinner weekends; **Closed Wednesday**.
Vegetarian, Gluten-free options

Belgian chef Amand has been running restaurants on Gozo and working to promote the island for longer than most people can remember. Nowadays, apart from nipping out from the kitchen to greet old clients he works mainly behind the scenes, with his welcoming daughter Caroline working front-of-house.

Qbajjar (*By-ar*) Bay is on the quieter outskirts of the busy resort of Marsalforn and the restaurant enjoys rural and sea views right opposite the Qbajjar slipway.

There are two menus – bistro and à la carte – as well as a list of specials changing to ensure fresh food on a daily basis. Items to look out for (some of the regulars say to die for) are his signature dishes: lobster bisque, a creamy seafood cannelloni, and a delicious sabayon... a Belgian variety of zabaglione.

Otherwise, there is a range of salads and of pastas, Angus rib-eye, chicken breast supreme, calamari, king prawns and local fish. Another speciality is his Flemish beef stew, made with beer and mustard. Desserts include mousse au chocolat, crepes and crème caramel, so it is obviously a spot at which to indulge yourself.

Cosy inside in winter; cool in summer
Seats 30 inside, 30 outside
Parking on street
Children and babies welcome

94 Country Terrace
2155-0248

Spectacular view

Price range: €21-40

Local, Italian

All major credit cards

Zewwieqa Street, **Mgarr**
Website: www.country-terrace.com
Open: 12-2.30pm; 6.30-10.30. **Closed Monday**
Vegetarian, Gluten-free, Lactose free meals available

Initially, at least, it is all about the view. A panorama taking in Blue Lagoon, across Comino and Cominotto and the northern coast of Malta, over to Fort Chambray and down to the Mgarr marina makes the setting unique. It has understandably become a favourite for wedding receptions and parties.

Patron Joseph Mercieca, known as Vigo, had a good track record as a popular restaurant manager before tastefully converting this former country club (it had been the summer home of a Maltese baron, with the best view in the Mediterranean) nearly ten years ago. His wife Kate works tirelessly but unobtrusively looking after the diners' needs.

The food is honest, local, basic and unpretentious (the most exotic dish probably being duck à l'orange), and features fresh mussels, prawns, meat or fish carpaccio, garlic mushrooms as starters and rabbit, eight types of pasta, steak, lamb or boneless quail to follow. Portions are generally generous (some people actually opt for the children's menu, or for starter-size main courses).

But it's the view to fall in love with and return to. Don't be surprised if it distracts you from the menu.

Air-conditioned inside
Seats 95 inside, 385 outside (for functions)
Parking on street
Children welcome; high chairs available;
Baby-changing facilities
Disabled access/WC.

LOUNGE BAR & RESTAURANT

We specialise in local and Italian cuisine
offering you the possibility to indulge in a large variety of
fresh fish, lamb, rabbit, game and more.
We guarantee that the variety is large enough
to tickle everyone's taste buds.

We are geared to cater large parties, weddings and outside catering.
Now also in Malta.

Zewwieqa Street - Mgarr - Gozo
For reservation please call Mob: 9944 6833 - Tel: 2155 0248
info@country-terrace.com - countryterracemgarr@gmail.com
www.country-terrace.com

96D-Bar
2155-6242
Sicilian, Maltese, Pizzeria
27 St Joseph Square, **Qala**
Website:
Open: Dinner, 6pm-10.30pm. **Closed Monday**
Lunch: Sat-Sun11.30-2pm;
Vegetarian, Gluten-free options

Island favourite
Price range: €16-34
AmEx, M/C, Visa

The queue of traffic outside this popular family-run corner bar and restaurant is testament to the renowned quality of the take-away pizzas for which people drive from all corners of the island. But now there is more than the 16 pizzas – you can order anything on the menu as a take-away.

Although essentially a local bar it has become popular with foreign residents and is always fairly quickly discovered by tourists.

It is usually busy, so standing at the bar (draught Guinness and lager) can sometimes involve a longish wait, but the emphasis thereafter is on good service, good food and value for money. Don't come here to eat unless you are hungry, for the portions can be challenging; try the D-Bar Special Pizza which comes laden with all the other favourite toppings, or the hefty lamb shanks and the gargantuan spare ribs.

In addition to the set menu there are usually daily specials – half a dozen choices of both starters and main courses –including fresh fish and sometimes a mild chicken or lamb curry. Desserts are all home-made.

Whether ordering a table or a take-away, be sure to ring ahead.

Air-conditioned
Seats 80 inside, 24 outside
Parking in church square, opposite
Children welcome; high chairs available
Dress: Any

Tad Dutch

Village square favourite

2722-4224

Price range: €19-36

Dutch, Mediterranean
St Joseph Square, **Qala**
Website
Open: Dinner from 6pm. **Closed Thursday**
Vegetarian, Gluten-free, Lactose-free, Vegan dishes available

It was a tapas bar; now, as its name suggests, it is predominantly Dutch, which is also the nationality of the chef, Mireille; Katia, front of house, is a local girl. (It's still possible to concoct your own version of tapas – slightly different ingredients – with a personal selection from the starters menu.)

Mireille cooks with passion, concentrating on locally produced food and home-made products. Her background means that she understands the need for different – warmer – dishes in the 'shoulder' and winter months. But the summer menu is equally well conceived.

Starters could be pasta, salad, soup or even whelks; mains, a lamb tenderloin, a juicy entrecote or the highly rated tender calf's liver; an Indonesian curry (the Dutch influence) or maybe the *Stamppost* – pork loin, meatballs and pork belly with mashed potatoes. The bread is made to a Belgian recipe and although it's quite different is as delicious as local Gozo bread.

There is a selection of Dutch and Belgian beers including one made by Trappist monks – try it and you will understand why they can't talk.

Air conditioned
Seats 40 inside, 14 outside
Parking in church square, opposite
Dress code: casual
Babies and children welcome

Fliegu
2155-0055
Local and Sicilian
Triq L'Mgarr, **Nadur**
Website
Open: 12-3pm; 6-10pm. **Closed Tuesday**
Vegetarian, Gluten-free

Greatest panoramic view
Price range: €12-42
All major credit cards

The name *(flee-goo)* means Channel or Strait, and that is the view it commands – across the small farms and countryside of the south coast, over to Mgarr Harbour, the beautiful blue Channel into Blue Lagoon and beyond Comino to Malta.

The view strikes you as you enter the bar; stop for a drink while considering the menu and look through the internal window onto and beyond the kitchen with its wood-burning pizza oven. It must be the best outlook of any kitchen anywhere.

Eat inside, air-conditioned, with big picture windows or upstairs on the open terrace (sheltered against the wind and cosily heated in cooler seasons) under the caring and constantly smiling attention of hosts Tony and Vanessa Grech.

Pizza, prepared to his own recipe by a Sicilian chef, is the speciality of the house and there are about forty different varieties, but tender steaks have also become a popular feature and now there is also a Sicilian meat chef.

Diners can choose their wines from a walk-in wine cellar featuring more than 100 local and foreign labels.

Air conditioning
Seats 96 inside; 64 on the terrace
Parking: on street
Babies and children welcome: high chairs
Wheelchair accessible and disabled WC
Dress code: Casual.

Ta' Frenc

Fine dining: Country

2155-3888

Price range: €35-60

International, Mediterranean

All major credit cards

Triq Ghajn Damma, off the Marsalforn Road (**Marsalforn**)
Website: www.tafrencrestaurant.com
Open: 12-2pm, 6-10pm. **Closed Tuesday**
(Jan-Mar: open Fri, Sat lunch & dinner and Sunday lunch)
Vegetarian, Gluten-free, meals available

Voted by diners as the best restaurant on the Maltese islands, this converted 14th-century farmhouse halfway between Victoria and the coast is the benchmark for fine dining and consequently where locals go for special occasions. But the introduction of a fixed-price 'market menu' means that they can also come for no reason – except the food.

Friends meet for cocktails on the delightfully fragrant front terrace beside a garden producing herbs and citrus fruits for the kitchen (and for herb-scented teas as a digestif). Inside, specialities include flambé dishes (including seafood pasta flamed with Ricard or steak diane and concluding with crèpes suzette), delicious local pork in three forms, and a chateaubriand perfectly cooked and carved at the table for two people. Fresh fish is supplied daily by local fishermen. Ta' Frenc has its own source for chicken, quail and rabbit, as well as for olive oil, Champagne and cognac. The restaurant features a regular series of speciality dinners with emeritus chef Mario Schembri's highly-tuned brigade often being assisted by Michelin-starred chefs from Sicily, Italy or France. There is an award-winning selection of fine wines – local, classic and new world – from a temperature-controlled cellar that can be hired for private functions. It is also hugely popular for smart summer weddings (which can be performed on-site) with receptions on the large terrace.

Air-conditioned
Seats 60 inside, 120 outside
Dress code: Smart-casual.
High chairs and baby-changing facilities.

Jeffrey's
2156-1006
Local

Local favourite

Price range: €16-42
All major credit cards

Gharb Street, **Gharb**
Website:
Open: Daily (Summer) 6-10pm
Vegetarian, Gluten-free options

At the end of the newish main road from Victoria, where it forks to head for Gharb and San Lawrenz and next to a red telephone kiosk. Chef-patron Joe Sultana's lease ran out just after the road did and he moved across it and downsized immediately opposite. A landmark venue in more senses than one.

Restaurants are at a premium at this end of the island and Joe closes from November to March, so his regulars get to eat there only when it is packed with tourists. And now it is a much smaller space (you might want to ask him to turn down the volume on the TV set.)

But note... it seats only about 12 people.

The basic menu remains much as before: sensible plain food, well prepared and cheerfully presented – salads, pastas, rabbit, bragioli, lamb shanks, beef pancake, stuffed marrows... sometimes a curry.

There's a large but rarely seen multinational ex-pat community in Gharb. They use Jeffrey's in order to avoid the need to traverse Victoria for a meal elsewhere. More tellingly, people will wriggle through the capital in the opposite direction just to get there to eat. It's worth the effort.

But book.

Air-conditioned
Seats 12
Parking on street
Dress: Any
Children and babies welcome: children's menu

Il-Kantra Lido Bar & Rastaurant
2219-1000

Sicilian   **All major credit cards**

Mgarr-ix-Xini, **Sannat**
Website: www.tacenc.com
Open: 12-3.30pm; 7-10.30pm
Vegetarian, Gluten-free, meals available

Overlooking the mouth of a sheltered bay that was once used by the Knights as a landing place (the address means harbour of the galleys), this splendid open-air restaurant is the latest addition to the five-star Hotel Ta'Cenc complex.

It commands a view across the water to the Knight's tower, built on the opposite headland as a result of the corsair raid of 1551, and across to Comino and Malta.

It is a bar and grill restaurant serving drinks or meals: fresh fish, grilled meats, pastas, a variety of salads and other favourites in the magnificent surroundings of Kantra Beach.

As its name suggests it is a place for relaxing as well as for eating and drinking: sun beds and umbrellas are part of the furniture.

Ta'Karolina
2155-9675
Mediterranean, Local
Marina Street, **Xlendi**
Open: Daily, 12-3pm; 6.30pm-10.30 (winter: lunch only)

Tucked away, almost hidden, at the foot of the Xlendi cliffs, it is the last in a row of three waterside restaurants – you need to walk through the other two to reach it. It is named after the saintly Karolina Cauchi, a well-to-do local woman who became a nun and founded the Dominican sisters who gathered in a cave where the restaurant now stands.

There, right in the corner, it has something that might be unique – its own private beach (if you could call a patch of golden sand that would be filled if two people sat on it, a 'beach'). But it is a memento of the time when Xlendi Bay was a women-only swimming area: no men, not even fishermen, allowed.

The frequently returning clientele is testament to the excellent food, friendly service and relaxed ambiance of this popular restaurant. Local favourites such as *aljotta* (fish soup) and rabbit are available, as are pizzas and pastas, rib-eye steaks, pork loin and fresh seafood.

There is also a small range of platters for two diners to share: fish, Italian cold cuts or mixed cheeses

Seats 40 inside; 75 outside
Parking nearby
Dress: Any
Children and babies welcome: high chairs available
Baby-changing facilities available
Wheelchair access and WC facilities

Kartell

Water's edge

2155-6918

Price range: €21-37

Local, Mediterranean

All major credit cards

Marina street, **Marsalforn**
Website: www.il-kartellrestaurant.com
Open: daily, 11.30-3.30, 6pm-10.30. **Closed Wednesday (Nov-April)**
Vegetarian, Gluten-free, meals available

Hugely prominent (most days, just look for the crowd) in the left-hand corner of the bay in the island's most popular resort, this restaurant has been a favourite for more than forty years – and deservedly so.

It used to specialise in pizza, with the first genuine Italian wood-burning oven, but fish nowadays dominates the menu and once you have made your choice from the variety on the platter presented to you the waiters will discuss with you the different ways in which it can be cooked.

However busy they are, the staff give the impression that they are interested in what you want and find time to discuss the food as well as the drink to accompany it.

The family recently expanded its own vineyard, so there is a good range of own-label wines, as well as home-pressed olive oil, to tempt the palate. Fresh fruit and vegetables come from the family's estate.

In winter there is plenty of warm and comfortable heated accommodation indoors. But the best place to be is outside with the sea lapping beside your table and a great view across the bay.

Seats 80 inside, 120 outside
Parking in car park nearby
Children welcome; high chairs available
Baby-changing facilities
Disabled access/WC

Il-Kcina tal-Barrakka
2155-6543

Fishermen's favourite
Price range: €22-33

Maltese and Mediterranean
Manoel De Vilhena Street, **Mgarr**
Website:
Open: 7pm-10.30. Sundays noon-10.30pm. **Closed Monday**
Vegetarian, Gluten-free meals available

Better known as Sammy's, and everybody has heard of Sammy's; it has been the fish-lovers' favourite eating place for more than three decades. *Luzzu* fishermen come back to the harbour to eat the fish they caught that day – can there be a greater accolade than that? The fishermen sit and talk about local politics while on the next table there may be a couple of government ministers talking about the fish.

So the *Kcina* (*Kit-cheena*) revolves around seafood and the array of fresh fish on offer changes daily, and sometimes even during the evening as more boats come in and tie up: mussels, prawns, shrimps, tuna, barracuda and swordfish, Mediterranean sole, sea bass and sea bream, lobsters, squid, sea urchins and crayfish, John Dory and amberjack: and towards the end of summer the ubiquitous *lampuki*.

Cevice (marinated raw fish) or *aljotta* (fish soup) is the way most people start. But for non-fish eaters, and because the fishermen are not always so lucky, there are meat options available, notably tender fillets of beef, duck or lamb, and sometimes a mild chicken curry. The desserts are all home made.

This summer the restaurant was getting up-to-date with the installation of a machine for credit cards, and there are plans to increase the size of the tables.

Seats 58 outside
Parking nearby
Dress: casual.

SAMMY'S
Il-Kċina tal-Barrakka
Restaurant

Specialising in Seafood

For reservation please call:
Tel: **2155 6543** · **9921 3801** · **7959 2952**

28, Manuel De Vilhena Str., Mgarr, Gozo, Malta.

110 Mediterranean Breeze
2156-3840

Fantastic view

Price range: €25-33

All major credit cards

Mediterranean
Grand Hotel, **Mgarr**
Website: www.grandhotelmalta.com
Open Daily: Dinner, summer only.
Vegetarian, Gluten-free, meals available

Scorchingly hot during the day, so open only towards sunset, this spacious rooftop restaurant at the four-star Grand Hotel commands one of the very best views of the harbour, the Channel, and Comino, and across to Malta. It is also a terrific spot from which to watch the fireworks at most of the village festas around the island.

The hotel's chefs offer a fine selection of mouth watering antipasto, with live cooking and grill – the roof is a long way from the kitchen so there is a fair amount of barbecue cooking.

As in the hotel's main ground floor restaurant, the emphasis is generally on Mediterranean menus with essentially local produce that may include barley-reared lamb.

In addition the chef organises 'theme' menus that might be Italian, Maltese or even Thai.

111Il-Migiarro
2156-3840

Mediterranean
Grand Hotel, **Mgarr**
Website: www.grandhotelmalta.com
Open: Daily: Breakfast, Lunch, Dinner.
Vegetarian, Gluten-free, meals available

4* Hotel dining
Price range: €25-33
All major credit cards

Huge windows in the spacious main dining room provide a wonderfully uninterrupted panoramic view over the bustling harbour, Comino, Fort Chambray and the northern coast of Malta. There are buffets and à la carte in the dining room in winter and the shoulder months, barbecues on the terrace in summer, bar snacks on the terrace for lunch all year round. Wherever you sit, the staff will be smiling, attentive, helpful, and the food as you would expect from an underrated four-star hotel.

There is usually a choice of four main meat dishes, plus fish, to follow a mouth-watering range of antipasti. But the menu is less reliant than some places on frozen food, so the menu is consequently relatively short. Try the duck breast and chicken terrine, local pork fillet wrapped in parma ham with tarragon and cream sauce for a main and the white chocolate panna cotta with forest fruit coulis for dessert.

Three brothers – owner Silvio, manager Renato and banqueting manager Alfio – have found a winning formula that attracts people back year after year from all corners of the world. Day visitors can sit on the terrace and watch for the arrival of the ferry and then walk fairly leisurely downhill for the return trip to Malta.

Air conditioning
Seating: 100 inside, 40 outside
Underground car park
Babies and children welcome. High chairs
Dress code: Smart casual
Disabled access, WC

112 Oleander
2155-7230
Local
Victory Square, **Xaghra**
Website:
Open: 12-3pm; 6pm-10.00. **Closed Monday**
Vegetarian, Gluten-free options

Home cooking
Price range: €12-27
All major credit cards

When they are not cooking at home this is a long-time favourite place for Gozitans and Maltese to come for what they consider to be the ultimate version of local 'home cooking', but in a restaurant. The village is a major hub of the island and the range of restaurants in the square makes it one of the busiest. So cars are not only racing through, they are parking… just about anywhere they like.

The menu that attracts the diners (and as many are turned away as are seated, because they have failed to book) starts with traditional fish soup, goes through pasta, home-made ravioli and rabbit stew or local lamb to quail, chicken, duck and steaks.

With a bit of judicious shuffling they reckon to be able to seat 70 in summer in the square under the umbrellas and red-and-white oleander trees. Inside the 300-year-old building is an arched limestone-ceilinged dining room that is comfortable and cosy on cooler nights.

If you want to sample Goozitan cooking before you leave the island – and of course you should – this is the place for it.

But book.

Air-conditioned inside
Seats 40 inside, 70 outside
Parking in square
Children welcome; high chairs available
Dress: Any
Wheelchair access.

L'Ortolan
2211 0000

Fine dining: Country
Price Range: €50-63
All major credit cards

Mediterranean
Kempinski Hotel, **San Lawrenz**
Website: www.kempinski.com/en/gozo
Open Daily: 6.30-10pm
Vegetarian, Gluten-free, Lactose-free meals available

Elegant, but expensive; unless you are already staying at the luxurious five-star international hotel with dinner included in the half-board tariff, this is a place that is likely to be reserved for special occasions. For you are dining in style.

Approached by a grand wooden staircase—fine carpentry is much in evidence at the hotel which is said to be fashioned in the style of an old-fashioned hunting lodge – the restaurant's large terrace looks across the swimming pools to open countryside and on to the attractive Dwerja Bay in the distance.

The menu is of the calibre you might expect, and possibly better, with starters like roast breast of pigeon, or a pressed terrine of oxtail and foie gras... supreme of pheasant or saddle of wild boar for mains... chocolate and cherry crème brulée or banana, coffee and brandy tiramisu to finish.

There is always a choice of vegetarian options and gluten and lactose allergies can be catered for. It is, after all, a five star Kempinski.

Air-conditioned inside
Seats 75 inside, 75 outside
Hotel car park
Dress code: Smart casual.
Babies and children welcome; high chairs
Wheelchair access and WC facilities

114 Patrick's

2156-6667

Steak house, Wine bar, International cuisine
Europe Street, **Victoria**
Website: www.patrickstmun.com
Open: 6.30-10.30pm. **Closed: Sunday**
(Winter: Sunday lunch: 12.30-2.30pm. **Closed Sunday night, Monday**)
Vegetarian, Gluten-free, Lactose-free meals available

Fine dining: City
Price range: €28-58
All major credit cards

Step into the cool elegance of this multi-award-winning restaurant along a quiet street on the edge of Victoria and you could imagine you were about to dine in Milan, Paris or New York. Chef-patron Patrick Buttigieg offers a sophisticated and stylish decor with well-spaced tables, an engaging and knowledgeable staff and an unbeatable wine list, copies of which are available for diners who frequently ask to take it home to show friends.

However, it's the exceptional standard of food on which the restaurant's reputation is based. If undecided, consider the Chef's Tasting Menu, a mouth-watering selection of six courses complemented by a different glass of wine for each dish – it might be pan-seared foie gras, baby swordfish carpaccio, confit of duck leg and scallops. The à la carte menu offers soups with temptingly matched ingredients.

But the emphasis is on meat, so try Kobe beef carpaccio; Irish prime steer and Angus, Argentinean or even Kobe steaks; and there is also pork belly (a tender and juicy favourite), duck and lamb. On the non-meat side there will be black sea-bass and varieties of pasta. Desserts include chocolate fondant and crème brûlée.

And check out the award-winning wine list.

Air-conditioned. Seats 50
Parking on street
Dress: Smart casual.
Well-behaved children welcome.

PATRICK'S

Lounge, Restaurant & Steakhouse

+356 2156 6667 | www.patrickstmun.com | Triq l-Ewropa, Victoria, Gozo

116 Il-Panzier
2155-9979

Hidden city gem
Price range: €18-38
Most major credit cards

Sicilian
39, Charity Street, **Victoria**
Website:
Open:Daily, 12-2.30, 6.30-9.30
Vegetarian and Gluten-free specialities

The location, up a quiet narrow street on the left-hand side of St George's Basilica, does this restaurant no favours; the previous two owners had abandoned it as a hopeless case. But with typical Sicilian fortitude Valentino Valenti managed to turn the place around and into a successful and popular venture and venue.

The shady and narrow street leads up to a shady and narrow corridor, lined with wine, and onto an attractive courtyard with yucca and palm trees in the centre, the sides sheltered by a wooden roof that makes it a wind-free sun trap. In the height of summer water is pumped over the roof to keep it cool, creating a waterfall at the edges and the feeling of eating in a tropical rain-forest.

The tables and crockery are all hand-painted Sicilian ceramics in order to complement the menu and service. Try the saltimbocca (it means 'jumps in the mouth') or the house speciality of pork *al volcano*, which is minced pork cooked between lemon leaves. Alexandra in the kitchen changes the menu frequently according to the freshness of food available and everything is presented at the table with Sicilian charm by Valentino.

Cover charge: €1.40pp
Air-conditioned – outside
Seats: 52 outside
Parking: Main car park
Dress code: Casual.

117**Pings**
2156-6680

Chinese, South Indian
Fortunato Mizzi Street, **Victoria**
Website: www.pingsgozo.com
Open: 12-2pm; 6-10.30pm.**Closed Monday lunch**
Vegetarian, Gluten-free meals available

City: Tastes of Asia
Price range: €19-35
All major credit cards

This restaurant quickly became a hugely popular venue on the road to Xlendi, then relocated to the capital, Victoria, with an additional chef and a new menu extended to include 'south Indian' dishes which are happily very diverse. Curry lovers who don't know the geography will be pleased to learn that the region includes Madras (little known in India but describing a type of southern state curry) and, at a stretch, even Vindaloo (which is more accurately from Goa, on the west coast).

The Chinese favourites remain, with Peking Duck (of course), wontons, dim sum, dumplings and spring rolls, sweet-and-sour, and a range of sizzling, battered, or wok-fried meat or vegetarian dishes, plus the usual fried rice or 'Singapore' noodles.

As a bonus for geographers, there's also Japanese seafood soup, Korean-style duck, Thai beef or chicken, Mongolian-style lamb, and Malaysian satay.

Service is excellent, friendly and attentive.

Take-aways are available.

Air-conditioned
Seats 60
Parking on street
Dress: casual
Babies and children welcome; high chairs

118 Porto Vecchio

2156-3317

Terrific location
Price range: €16-34
All major credit cards

Italian, Local
Yacht Marina, **Mgarr**
Website: www.portovecchiorestaurant.com
Open: 12-3pm; 7-10.30pm. **Closed Wednesday**
Vegetarian, Gluten-free, Lactose-free meals available

To be any closer to the harbour than the terrace of this restaurant you would need to be afloat. You are there in it and among it, virtually between the yacht masts as if on the upper deck of a luxury pleasure cruiser, only with a higher and better view above and through the thick glass 'wall'. You are an honorary yottie.

Service is first class. The à la carte menu is Italian-biased (the full name of the restaurant is *Ristorante* Porto Vecchio). It contains all the standard fare – soups, antipasto, pasta, rice and meat dishes – but, with little reliance on the freezer is commendably short. What matters, what the regulars go for, are the specials which change daily according to the freshness of the food in the market and the success of the fishermen's daily catch. If it's available, try the tuna tartare as a mouth-watering starter. And the tuna steak itself cuts like butter – delicious.

Father and son team Chris and Walter-John Cassar created and designed this restaurant and have made it a total success. Nothing, it seems, is too much trouble for them in catering for their appreciative clientele.

It might be the location that first attracts the diners, but it's the quality of food and service that keeps them coming back.

Air-conditioned
Seats 65 inside; 75 outside
Parking on street, and car park
Dress: casual
Babies and children welcome; high chairs, baby-changing facilities
Wheelchair accessible and WC

Martino Garzes Str,
Yacht Marina, Mgarr,
GSM 2413, Gozo - Malta

T +356 2156 3317
M +356 9944 4999
E portovecchiogozo@gmail.com
W www.portovecchiorestaurant.com

RISTORANTE E VINOTECA

Opening hours: Daily lunch 12.00 to 3.00pm
Dinner: 7.00pm to 10.00pm and closed on Wednesdays.

Ta' Ricardo *Historic site*

2155-5953

Gozitan All credit cards

4 triq il-Fosos, Citadella, **Victoria**

Open: Daily, 10am-6pm (later by request)

Vegetarian options

After searching for a place to park and then trekking back up the hill on which the Citadel stands, you are entitled to a drink. A clue for the place to do this is a barrel with a bottle and a couple of glasses on top at the entrance to Ricardo's on the steep street up the left hand side of the cathedral.

You'll be joined while you eat and drink by locals, tourists and lawyers from the nearby court building.

More a wine bar with food than a full-blown restaurant, it is a special sort of place — special enough, at least, for the tourist authority to steer foreign travel writers there to sample both history and 'genuine local fare'. In fact it is one of the old family homes from the days when Gozitans were required by law to spend every night inside the Citadel for safety. The arched main room has a stone staircase leading to an upper chamber with additional seating.

The menu is likely to feature local rabbit, goat, ravioli, or spaghetti with rabbit sauce; and for vegetarians local salads involving sun-dried tomatoes, soft and hard-peppered goat cheese, artichokes, capers and olives.

Wash it down with a glass or two of Ricardo's own Gozo wine to complete your experience of 'genuine local fare'.

Cool in summer; heated in winter

Seats 80

Parking is either impossible or dead lucky

Dress code: Any

Rew Rew
79-85-4007

Price range: varies daily
No credit cards

Mediterranean
Mgarr ix-Xini, **Sannat**
Open daily, 12-4pm. **Closed Dec-Feb**
Vegetarian meals available

Start with transport cafe-style (metal) chairs and tables. Then move it all outdoors into the sunshine. Add a beautiful bay – a fjord, actually – at the end of a spectacular deep terraced (vines and olives) valley with high cliffs of gold on either side. A pebble beach with a couple of colourful luzzu fishing boats bobbing alongside the jetty. The blue sea lapping virtually at your feet...

The name of the inlet means harbour of the galleys and was once a favoured shelter (at different times) for both Knights and pirates.

It used to be a locals' secret, but word has spread. Now there are Sicilians arriving by fast motor cruiser – they come over for lunch, drop anchor and row or swim in to the beach (the inner area is cordoned off as a swimmers-only zone). The menu is on a chalk board because food and prices vary daily according to the local catch and, fairly obviously, fish figures prominently; but there are also Black Angus steaks and beefburgers available. Everything is cooked on the barbecue.

More easily accessed by sea than by land, the bay is at the end of a steep heart-stopping road, mostly single-carriageway and mostly of farm-track standard, starting among farms between Xewkija and Sannat.

But it is worth looking for, and driving to, for Noel's skilled cooking. The Sicilians know a good restaurant when they find one.

Seats 50 outside.
Parking in Bay
Dress code: Casual
Children and babies welcome; high chairs

Sapana
2156-2100

Village Indian

Price range: €14-27

All major credit cards

Indian
5 Rabat Road, **Xlendi**
Website: sapanaindianrestaurant.com
Open: Dinner 6.30-11pm (**Winter: Closed Mon, Tues**)
Vegetarian, Gluten-free options

Formerly the Village Inn and specialising in English roast dinners, the restaurant changed ownership and menu and immediately became known as the Village Indian. But its new name means 'dream' in Hindi. It is appropriate because during the ten years he spent managing Asian restaurants for other people, it was owner Frankie's dream to open his own, and to offer excellent food allied with impeccable service.

The menu will be familiar to most European visitors. There are the usual starters – onion bhaji, samosas, kebabs and tandoori. And of course papadoms with a choice of dressing. Then Korma, Tikka Massala. Madras, Balti, Rogan Josh, Vindaloo. Tandoori and Gosht variations of chicken, beef, lamb and fish, and six varieties of rice.

The restaurant is bright and comfortable and in summer there are tables outside on the street (which is officially closed to traffic) affording a sea and sunset view. The kitchen window opens on to the street, so you can watch your meal being prepared.

Air-conditioned
Seats: 28 inside, 45 outside
Parking nearby
Children welcome; high chairs
Dress: Casual

123**Seaview**

2156-5541

Harbour view

Price range: €25-35

AmEx, Visa, M/C

Mediterranean, seafood, pizza

15 Shore Street, **Mgarr**

Website:

Open: lunch from 11.30am; dinner 6.30pm. **Closed Tuesday**

Vegetarian dishes available

Let's start with the seating. Their wicker armchairs on the terrace are the most comfortable on Gozo and possibly anywhere else. Then the view – it is along, rather than across, the marina, and takes in the fishing fleet, private motor cruisers and yachts moored there. And the ferry terminal, of course, which is almost close enough to touch.

That's before you get to the food. The restaurant is directly across the road from the jetty where the fishing boats come in and tie up. Nowhere could be closer, so fresh fish straight off the boat is the staple fare, usually presented to you on a tray from which to make a choice. But there are also meat dishes like rack of pork ribs, charcoal grilled fillet steak and local rabbit stew.

Starters include different forms of mixed antipasto.

On the ground floor, is the Pizza Marina – effectively a totally separate restaurant – which was completely refurbished this year. There is a choice of 20 different pizza toppings, in addition to burgers, omelettes, a Gozitan platter and an English breakfast. You can stay and dine on the street-level terrace or order your meal to take away,

Seats: 40 inside, 60 outside

Parking nearby

Children welcome; high chairs; kids' menu

Dress: Casual

AVAILABLE
NOW

REAL ALE
FROM
GOZO

LIGHT AND HOPPY
BREWED IN
GOZO

3.8% ABV

GOZBREWERY.COM

Sicilia Bella

2156-3588

Waterfront

Price range: €24-40

All major credit cards

Sicilian

Manoel de Valhena Street, **Mgarr**

Website:

Open: 12-3pm, 6-10.30pm. **Closed Monday**

March-June: Lunch Sat and Sun only

Vegetarian, Gluten free meals available

This friendly _ristorante_ is the first you come to on the harbour and has a good view of the business of the port, from the coming and going of the ferries to the traffic-stopping meandering of a family of ducks. The island's first customs house, it was built by the Knights in 1733 and has a square wooden-beamed dining room and small bar – although diners will want to sit on the terrace with the view.

Fish is of course as fresh as can be and regulars go for the chef's platter which contains a dozen varieties of seafood (sometimes more): it varies according to the daily catch but usually includes calamari, mussels and local prawns.

There are ten different types of pasta, and fish courses including calamari stuffed with spinach, salmon and prawns, then a range of meat dishes – stuffed pork chops, grilled lamb cutlets, chicken and steaks. In addition there are always daily specials. The tasty Italian desserts are all home made, and there will be good espresso, and maybe a house _limoncello_ to round off your meal.

Seats 45 inside, 60 outside

Parking nearby

Dress code: any

Babies and children welcome: high chairs; children's menu

126 Tatita's
2156-6482

Italian, Local
St Lawrence Square, **San Lawrenz**
Website:
Open: 12-3pm, 6-10.30pm. **Closed Tuesday**
Vegetarian, Gluten-free dishes available

Smart village square
Price range: €22-30
All major credit cards

Dine beneath umbrellas and oleander trees in the recently tiled and embellished village square. San Lawrenz has been undergoing a total renovation, including the facade of the parish church and – even more importantly for visiting diners – the completion of the long-awaited access road which is the main 'trunk' road from Victoria (take the left fork at the entrance to Gharb).

Tatita's is a clean crisp white bright and modern family-run restaurant, especially popular among residents of the Kempinski Hotel who can manage it in a short and easy walk.

Fish, usually from boats operating from the nearby Inland Sea, predominates on the menu and lobster, when available, is highly rated, but there are also speciality local dishes including rabbit and bragioli.

In addition to the à la carte there's usually a daily specials menu at €22 featuring a choice of three options each for starters man and desserts.

Air-conditioned
Seats: 40 inside; 75 outside
Parking in square
Dress code: smart casual
Babies and children welcome; high chairs; children's menu

It-Tokk *City square people-watching*

2155-1213

Coffee bar and restaurant: Local and Mediterranean fare
Independence Square, **Victoria**
Website:
Open: 10am-10pm. **Closed Sunday**
Vegetarian, Gluten free options

Eat inside or among the hawkers' stalls at a table in a corner of the busy square from which this restaurant and coffee bar takes its name, or on the shaded upper terrace commanding an excellent view of the hustle and bustle beneath and of the Citadel beyond it, especially during the morning when the market is at its busiest.

It is much calmer and quieter in the afternoons when most of the locals are enjoying their siesta.

It's also a great spot to watch the organised functions of the city centre at any time – Carnival, St George's feast and Santa Marija, *Notte Gozitan*a – as well as the relatively disorganised activities that go on non-stop.

The menu is predominantly local, featuring such Gozitan favourites as a hearty fish soup (with delicious crusty local bread), rabbit stew, fresh fish, bragioli and pizza and a Gozitan cheese platter They also serve a full English breakfast all day.

A genuine favourite for genuine local food, with genuinely friendly service.

Parking: main car park
Babies and children welcome.
Dress code: Any

Tmun – Mgarr
2156-6276

Fine dining; Waterfront
Price range: €24-44
All major credit cards

Italian, Local, Mediterranean
Martino Garces Street, **Mgarr**
Website: www.tmunmgarr.com
Open: 12-2.30pm; 6.30-10.30. **Closed Tuesday**
Vegetarian, Gluten-free, meals available

A favourite of visitors and locals for more than 25 years, Tmun (formerly at Xlendi) is nowadays tucked away on the new marina road behind a row of colourful Gozitan fishing boats drawn up from the shimmering sea onto what is (one day) going to be an attractive piazza.

Leli – the restaurant is probably better known as 'Leli's' – is the supreme front-of-house man and oversees a team of outstandingly friendly and attentive waiting staff. Wife Jane, best fish cook on the island (she also does a great rack of lamb), created the dishes and son Paul has inherited her passion and developed her range. He works behind a window in full view of the diners – a sure sign of confidence. A choice of meat dishes is available but fish has always been the speciality, usually grilled or cooked *cartoccio* (in foil with oil, wine and herbs). And with local fishermen constantly padding barefoot across the street to deliver their daily catch it could hardly be fresher. The bouillabaisse with seven types of fish, served for two to share, has been a constant preference for regulars. As has Jane's delightful cheesecake and the array of home-made ice creams.

The new location means that Maltese regulars who used to drive to Xlendi for lunch can now leave their cars in Cirkewwa and walk from the ferry. It is usually, and deservedly, busy. So book.

Air-conditioned inside
Seats 30 inside, 40 outside (covered and heated in winter)
Parking on street
Dress code: Smart-casual.
Children and babies welcome; high chairs.

Ta' Tona
2156-1967

Harbour favourite

Price range: €18-41

All major credit cards

Local and Mediterranean
Manoel de Vilhena Street, **Mgarr**
Open: Lunch, Fri, Sat, Sun, Mon.
Dinner, daily 6pm-11pm. ; **Closed Tuesday**
Vegetarian and Gluten-free options

People usually mention the friendly, helpful and caring attitude of the waiters, as well as the excellence of the cooking. The staff take time to explain the menu and to make recommendations of both food and wine.

It is a family-run affair, with a family atmosphere. It has been operating since 1946 when it was little more than a cave where fishermen went for early morning coffee and to which they then sometimes returned to mend their nets and cook their catch over driftwood. It was obvious that members of the public would one day want to join them.

Fishermen still meet there to eat, and still mend their nets beside it, so fish figures large on the menu: fish soup, fresh mussels, fried fresh calamari (or occasionally baby calamari grilled with wine, garlic and basil), marinated octopus, local king prawns flamed with brandy... or a plate of seven types of fish... ten varieties of pasta, also available as a main course... steaks, lamb chops, pork fillets, rabbit... Given a day's notice they can usually provide lobster.

Desserts are home made, and change frequently. There's a good range of local and foreign wines.

And it's all served with a smile.

Seats 20 inside, 68 outside
Children welcome: high chairs
Parking in square
Dress casual

131 **Zafiro**

Seafront hotel

2156-5555

Price range: €23-41

Local and Mediterranean

All major credit cards

San Andrea Hotel, Seafront, **Xlendi**
Website: www.hotelsanandrea.com
Open daily: breakfast 8-10am; lunch 11-3pm; dinner 6-9.30
Vegetarian, Gluten free options

The ground floor and terrace restaurant of this (relatively) quiet three-star family-run hotel is in the corner of one of the island's most popular bays and commands a view between cliffs out to the Mediterranean that is particularly appealing at sunset with the sea gently lapping almost literally at your feet.

The à la carte menu offers a mouth-watering variety of fresh pasta, meat ,fish or Gozitan antipasti, a selection of fresh fish, shellfish, lobster (when available), grilled premium quality Irish or American steaks and other meat dishes including osso bucco, crispy duck and boned quail.

In addition there are daily specials featuring fresh fish and meat and market vegetables, salads and pasta; sometimes beef olives or pork medallions in a sweet and sour sauce.

The English breakfast – everything is available to non-residents – is highly praised by hotel guests, casual tourists and locals.

Air-conditioned
Seats: 80 inside: 50 outside
Parking: behind hotel
Babies and children welcome: high chairs
Dress: Casual